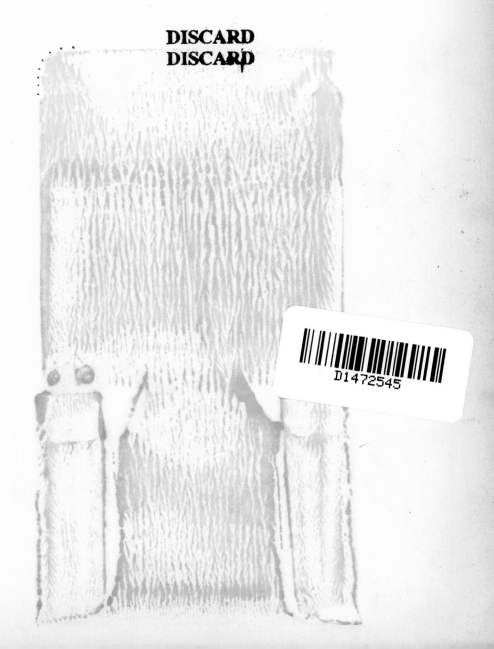

CHAMPLAIN COLLEGE

Discussions of Henrik Ibsen

DISCUSSIONS OF LITERATURE

General Editor JOSEPH H. SUMMERS, Washington University

Edited by

WORKS

The Canterbury Tales	CHARLES A. OWEN, JR., University of Connecticut
The Divine Comedy	IRMA BRANDEIS, Bard College
Hamlet	J. C. LEVENSON, University of Minnesota
Moby-Dick	MILTON R. STERN, University of Connecticut
Shakespeare's Histories	R. J. DORIUS, University of Hamburg
Shakespeare's Problem Comedies	ROBERT ORNSTEIN, University of Illinois
Shakespeare's Roman Plays	MAURICE CHARNEY, Rutgers University
Shakespeare's Sonnets	BARBARA HERRNSTEIN, Bennington College

AUTHORS

Jane Austen	WILLIAM HEATH, Amherst College
William Blake	JOHN E. GRANT, University of Connecticut
Charles Dickens	WILLIAM ROSS CLARK, University of Connecticut
John Donne	FRANK KERMODE, University of Manchester
George Eliot	RICHARD STANG, Washington University, St. Louis
Henrik Ibsen	JAMES WALTER MCFARLANE, King's College, University of Durham
Henry James	NAOMI LEBOWITZ, Washington University, St. Louis
Alexander Pope	RUFUS A. BLANSHARD, University of Connecticut
Jonathan Swift	JOHN TRAUGOTT, University of California, Berkeley
Mark Twain	GUY A. CARDWELL, Washington University, St. Louis
William Wordsworth	JACK M. DAVIS, University of Connecticut

GENRES

Modern American Drama	WALTER MESERVE, University of Kansas
Poetry: Form and Structure	FRANCIS MURPHY, Smith College
Poetry: Rhythm and Sound	GEORGE HEMPHILL, University of Connecticut
The Novel	ROGER SALE, University of Washington
The Short Story	HOLLIS SUMMERS, Ohio University

DISCUSSIONS

OF

HENRIK IBSEN

Edited with an Introduction by

James Walter McFarlane

KING'S COLLEGE, UNIVERSITY OF DURHAM

NEWCASTLE UPON TYNE

D. C. Heath and Company

BOSTON

Printed June 1966

CONTENTS

I

II

III

IN a sense, this selection of Ibsen criticism is self-introducing, for the first four items rehearse in general terms most of the traditional and many of the newer arguments that attach to the discussion of Ibsen and Ibsenism. The two opening pieces draw up the main co-ordinates of debate: the Shavian axis (with its direction immediately apparent in the title its author gave it), which made a claim on behalf of the plays as embodiments of a lesson, as illustrations of a thesis, as expressions of opinion, as exercises in moral persuasion; and what we can conveniently if a little eccentrically call the Menckian axis, which, incorporating the inevitable reaction, set out to discredit the Ibsen legend as it had taken shape, dismissed the "ideas" as commonplace, denied that Ibsen had any interest in the propagation of ethical notions, and stressed instead his preoccupation with the technical difficulties of dramatic composition.

These two points of view mark out an area in which there is a great deal of room for manoeuvre. The third and fourth pieces, by Bentley and McFarlane, briefly survey some of the moves that have been made over this ground, paying particular attention to the trends and developments in Ibsen criticism since 1945. These more recent years have seen a very substantial shift in the *kind* of attention paid to Ibsen, a shift that Ronald Peacock (whose "Effects of Ibsen" is the last item in this volume) has drawn attention to: in the preface to the American paperback edition of *The Poet in the Theatre* (Hill and Wang, 1960) he comments on the reinforcement which time has given to his phrases since their first appearance in print fourteen years earlier. Emphasizing that he had gone out of his way

in the original publication to stress that the enormous influence of the "social" plays had prevented a greater knowledge and understanding of Ibsen's work as a whole, he now adds: "I think I was right about this. In the postwar period a number of excellent studies have appeared which correct previous one-sided views. Above all, the shift of interest toward the psychological and symbolic later plays is noteworthy, because it runs parallel to the success of new poetic styles in the postwar theatre. It is not too much to say that the growth of the poetic movement has itself liberated the greater Ibsen; the change in taste it brought has opened our eyes again to the poet Ibsen who had stood in the shadow of the critic of society."

The six items in the next group, while exemplifying some of the more general ideas discussed in these introductory pieces, are more directly related to individual dramas. They have been arranged chronologically by date of composition of the work discussed, from *Love's Comedy* (1862) through *Brand* (1865) and *Peer Gynt* (1867), *Ghosts* (1881), *The Wild Duck* (1884), and *Hedda Gabler* (1890), to Ibsen's last work, *When We Dead Awaken* (1899). Thus the essays deal with Ibsen's early and middle works in addition to the rather more familiar works of the last quarter of the nineteenth century, and they cast light on what Ronald Peacock called "the greater Ibsen": they consider the verse dramas as well as the prose, Ibsen's comic genius as well as his serious side, and his symbolical and visionary works as well as the more orthodoxly realistic.

The last group of items considers Ibsenism in its wider aspects and from a number of different points of view—stylistic, comparative, influential. The special problem of what Ibsen has meant to later generations of playwrights is more particularly touched on in the last two selections.

Ibsenism (in all its changing senses) is a comparatively recent phenomenon, and most of the relevant discussion has taken place in the last seventy years. The essays here included are distributed fairly widely over the years, and the contributors come from both the older and newer generations of critics, from the ranks of "creative" writers, "free-lance" critics, and the more traditional scholars. If one assigns the nationalities rather arbitrarily, the critics represented here include five Americans, six Englishmen, two Irishmen, one Welshman, one Anglo-Dane, one Norwegian, and one Austrian. The book thus presents, it is hoped, something of the astonishingly wide range of critical approach that Ibsen has received.

The standard English-language edition of Ibsen's works has up to now been the *Collected Works* in twelve volumes, edited by William Archer. This will eventually be superseded by *The Oxford Ibsen* in eight volumes (Volumes 5 and 6 of which have already appeared), which will include new translations of all the plays and of Ibsen's notes, jottings, scenarios, and draft versions, as well as full bibliographical and other background information. Other useful omnibus English-language versions are those by Una Ellis-Fermor, Eva Le Gallienne, and Michael Meyer. The present standard biography is that by Halvdan Koht, *The Life of Ibsen* (English translation in two volumes, 1931). Other recommended works of criticism or commentary written in English but not represented in this selection are: Hermann J. Weigand, *The Modern Ibsen* (New York, 1925); Adolph E. Zucker, *Ibsen, the Master Builder* (New York, 1929); Brian W. Downs, *Ibsen: the Intellectual Background* (Cambridge, 1936); P. F. D. Tennant, *Ibsen's Dramatic Technique* (Cambridge, 1948); Janko Javrin, *Ibsen: An Approach* (London, 1950); John Northam, *Ibsen's Dramatic Method* (London, 1953); Eva Le Gallienne, prefaces to her translations of *Hedda Gabler* (1955) and *The Master Builder* (1955).

JAMES WALTER MCFARLANE

Discussions of Henrik Ibsen

Henrik Ibsen

George Bernard Shaw

The Lesson of the Plays

IN FOLLOWING this sketch of the plays written by Ibsen to illustrate his thesis that the real slavery of today is slavery to ideals of goodness, it may be that readers who have conned Ibsen through idealist spectacles have wondered that I could so pervert the utterances of a great poet. Indeed I know already that many of those who are most fascinated by the poetry of the plays will plead for any explanation of them rather than that given by Ibsen himself in the plainest terms through the mouths of Mrs. Alving, Relling, and the rest. No great writer uses his skill to conceal his meaning. There is a tale by a famous Scotch storyteller which would have suited Ibsen exactly if he had hit on it first. Jeanie Deans sacrificing her sister's life on the scaffold to ideal truthfulness is far more horrible than the sacrifice in *Rosmersholm*; and the *deus ex machina* expedient by which Scott makes the end of his story agreeable is no solution of the ethical problem raised, but only a puerile evasion of it. He dared not, when it came to the point, allow Effie to be hanged for the sake of Jeanie's ideals.[1]

Nevertheless, if I were to pretend that Scott wrote *The Heart of Midlothian* to shew that people are led to do as mischievous, as unnatural, as murderous things by their religious and moral ideals as by their envy and ambition, it would be easy to confute me from the pages of the book itself. And Ibsen, like Scott, has made his opinion plain. If any one attempts to maintain that *Ghosts* is a polemic in favor of indissoluble monogamic marriage, or that *The Wild Duck* was written to inculcate that truth should be told for its own sake, they must burn the text of the plays if their contention is to stand. The reason that Scott's story is tolerated by those who shrink from *Ghosts* is not that it is less terrible, but that Scott's views are familiar to all well-brought-up ladies and gentlemen, whereas Ibsen's are for the moment so strange to them as to be unthinkable. He is so great a poet that the idealist finds himself in the dilemma of being unable to conceive that such a genius should have an ignoble meaning, and yet equally unable to conceive his

---

[1] The common-sense solution of the ethical problem has often been delivered by acclamation in the theatre. Many years ago I witnessed a performance of a melodrama founded on this story. After the painful trial scene, in which Jeanie Deans condemns her sister to death by refusing to swear to a perfectly innocent fiction, came a scene in the prison. "If it had been me," said the jailor, "I wad ha sworn a hole through an iron pot." The roar of applause which burst from the pit and gallery was thoroughly Ibsenist in sentiment. The speech, by the way, must have been a gag of the actor's: at all events I cannot find it in the acting edition of the play.

From *The Quintessence of Ibsenism*, Constable, London, 2nd ed., 1913; first published 1891. Reprinted by permission of The Public Trustee and The Society of Authors, London.

real meaning otherwise than as ignoble. Consequently he misses the meaning altogether in spite of Ibsen's explicit and circumstantial insistence on it, and proceeds to substitute a meaning congenial to his own ideal of nobility.

⌐Ibsen's deep sympathy with his idealist figures seems to countenance this confusion.⌐ Since it is on the weaknesses of the higher types of character that idealism seizes, his most tragic examples of vanity, selfishness, folly, and failure are not vulgar villains, but men who in an ordinary novel or melodrama would be heroes. Brand and Rosmer, who drive those they love to death, do so with all the fine airs of the Sophoclean or Shakespearean good man persecuted by Destiny. Hilda Wangel, who kills the Master Builder literally to amuse herself, is the most fascinating of sympathetic girl-heroines. The ordinary Philistine commits no such atrocities: he marries the woman he likes and lives with her more or less happily ever after; but that is not because he is greater than Brand or Rosmer: he is less. The idealist is a more dangerous animal than the Philistine just as a man is a more dangerous animal than a sheep. Though Brand virtually murdered his wife, I can understand many a woman, comfortably married to an amiable Philistine, reading the play and envying the victim her husband. For when Brand's wife, having made the sacrifice he has exacted, tells him that he was right; that she is happy now; that she sees God face to face; and then reminds him that "whoso sees Jehovah dies," he instinctively clasps his hands over her eyes; and that action raises him at once far above the criticism that sneers at idealism from beneath, instead of surveying it from the clear ether above, which can only be reached through its mists.

If, in my account of the plays, I have myself suggested false judgments by describing the errors of the idealists in the terms of the life they have risen above rather than in those of the life they fall short of, I can only plead, with but moderate disrespect for the general reader, that if I had done otherwise I should have failed wholly to make my exposition intelligible. Indeed accurate terms for realist morality, though they are to be found in the Bible, are so out of fashion and forgotten that in this very distinction between idealism and realism, I am forced to insist on a sense of the words which, had not Ibsen forced my hand, I should perhaps have conveyed otherwise, to avoid the conflict of many of its applications with the vernacular use of the words.

This, however, was a trifle compared to the difficulty which arose from our inveterate habit of labelling men with the abstract names of their qualities without the slightest reference to the underlying will which sets these qualities in action. At an anniversary celebration of the Paris Commune of 1871, I was struck by the fact that no speaker could find a eulogy for the Federals which would not have been equally appropriate to the peasants of La Vendée who fought for their tyrants against the French revolutionists, or to the Irishmen and Highlanders who fought for the Stuarts at the Boyne or Culloden. The statements that the slain members of the Commune were heroes who died for a noble ideal would have left a stranger quite as much in the dark about them as the counter statements, once common enough in our newspapers, that they were incendiaries and assassins. Our obituary notices are examples of the same ambiguity. Of all the public men lately deceased when Ibsenism was first discussed in England, none was made more interesting by strongly marked personal characteristics than the famous atheist orator Charles Bradlaugh. He was not in the least like any other notable member of the House of Commons. Yet when the obituary notices appeared, with the usual string of qualities: eloquence, determination, integrity, strong common-sense, and so on, it would have been possible, by merely expunging all names and other external details from these notices, to leave the reader entirely unable to say whether the subject of them was Gladstone, Lord Morley, William Stead, or any one else no more like Bradlaugh than Garibaldi or the late Cardinal Newman, whose obituary certificates of morality might nevertheless have been reprinted almost verbatim for the occasion without any gross incongruity. Bradlaugh had been the subject of many sorts of newspaper notices in his time. Thirty years ago, when the middle classes supposed him to be a revolutionist, the string of qualities which the press hung upon him were all evil ones, great stress being laid on the fact that as he was an atheist it would be an insult to God to admit him to Parliament. When it became apparent that he was an anti-socialist force in politics, he, without any recantation of his atheism, at once had the string of evil qualities exchanged for a rosary of good ones; but it is hardly necessary to add that neither the old badge nor the new could ever give any inquirer the least clue to the sort of man he actually was: he might have been Oliver Cromwell or Wat Tyler or Jack Cade, Penn or Wilberforce or Wellington, the late Mr. Hampden of flat-earth-theory notoriety or Proudhon or the Archbishop of Canterbury, for all the distinction such labels could give him one way or the other. The worthlessness of these abstract descriptions is recognized in practice every day. Tax a stranger before a crowd with being a thief, a coward, and a liar; and the crowd will suspend its judgment until you answer the question, "What's he done?" Attempt to take up a collection for him on the ground that he is an upright, fearless, high-principled hero; and the same question must be answered before a penny goes into the hat.

The reader must therefore discount those partialities which I have permitted myself to express in telling the stories of the plays. They are as much beside the mark as any other example of the sort of criticism which seeks to create an impression favorable or otherwise to Ibsen by simply pasting his characters all over with good or bad con-

duct marks. If any person cares to describe Hedda Gabler as a modern Lucretia who preferred death to dishonor, and Thea Elvsted as an abandoned perjured strumpet who deserted the man she had sworn before her God to love, honor, and obey until her death, the play contains conclusive evidence establishing both points. If the critic goes on to argue that as Ibsen manifestly means to recommend Thea's conduct above Hedda's by making the end happier for her, the moral of the play is a vicious one, that, again, cannot be gainsaid. If, on the other hand, *Ghosts* be defended, as the dramatic critic of *Piccadilly* did defend it, because it throws into divine relief the beautiful figure of the simple and pious Pastor Manders, the fatal compliment cannot be parried. When you have called Mrs. Alving an emancipated woman or an unprincipled one, Alving a debauchee or a victim of society, Nora a fearless and noble-hearted woman or a shocking little liar and an unnatural mother, Helmer a selfish hound or a model husband and father, according to your bias, you have said something which is at once true and false, and in both cases perfectly idle.

The statement that Ibsen's plays have an immoral tendency, is, in the sense in which it is used, quite true. Immorality does not necessarily imply mischievous conduct: it implies conduct, mischievous or not, which does not conform to current ideals. All religions begin with a revolt against morality, and perish when morality conquers them and stamps out such words as grace and sin, substituting for them morality and immorality. Bunyan places the town of Morality, with its respectable leading citizens Mr. Legality and Mr. Civility, close to the City of Destruction. In the United States today he would be imprisoned for this. Born as I was in the seventeenth century atmosphere of mid-nineteenth century Ireland, I can remember when men who talked about morality were suspected of reading Tom Paine, if not of being downright atheists. Ibsen's attack on morality is a symptom of the revival of religion, not of its extinction. He is on the side of the prophets in having devoted himself to shewing that the spirit or will of Man is constantly outgrowing the ideals, and that therefore thoughtless conformity to them is constantly producing results no less tragic than those which follow thoughtless violation of them. Thus the main effect of his plays is to keep before the public the importance of being always prepared to act immorally. He reminds men that they ought to be as careful how they yield to a temptation to tell the truth as to a temptation to hold their tongues, and he urges upon women who either cannot or will not marry that the inducements held out to them by society to preserve their virginity and refrain from motherhood, may be called temptations as logically as the inducements to the contrary held out by individuals and by their own temperaments, the practical decision depending on circumstances just as much as a decision between walking and taking a cab, however less trivial both the action and the circumstances may be. He protests against the ordinary assumption that there are certain moral institutions which justify all means used to maintain them, and insists that the supreme end shall be the inspired, eternal, ever growing one, not the external unchanging, artificial one; not the letter but the spirit; not the contract but the object of the contract; not the abstract law but the living will. And because the will to change our habits and thus defy morality arises before the intellect can reason out any racially beneficent purpose in the change, there is always an interval during which the individual can say no more than that he wants to behave immorally because he likes, and because he will feel constrained and unhappy if he acts otherwise. For this reason it is enormously important that we should "mind our own business" and let other people do as they like unless we can prove some damage beyond the shock to our feelings and prejudices. It is easy to put revolutionary cases in which it is so impossible to draw the line that they will always be decided in practice more or less by physical force; but for all ordinary purposes of government and social conduct the distinction is a common-sense one. The plain working truth is that it is not only good for people to be shocked occasionally, but absolutely necessary to the progress of society that they should be shocked pretty often. But it is not good for people to be garrotted occasionally, or at all. That is why it is a mistake to treat an atheist as you treat a garrotter, or to put "bad taste" on the footing of theft and murder. The need for freedom of evolution is the sole basis of toleration, the sole valid argument against Inquisitions and Censorships, the sole reason for not burning heretics and sending every eccentric person to the madhouse.

In short, our ideals, like the gods of old, are constantly demanding human sacrifices. Let none of them, says Ibsen, be placed above the obligation to prove itself worth the sacrifices it demands; and let everyone religiously refuse to sacrifice himself and others from the moment he loses his faith in the validity of the ideal. Of course it will be said here by incorrigibly slipshod readers that this, far from being immoral, is the highest morality; but I really will not waste further definition on those who will neither mean one thing or another by a word nor allow me to do so. Suffice it that among those who are not ridden by current ideals no question as to the ethical soundness of Ibsen's plays will ever arise; and among those who are so ridden his plays will be denounced as immoral, and cannot be defended against the accusation.

There can be no question as to the effect likely to be produced on an individual by his conversion from the ordinary acceptance of current ideals as safe standards of conduct, to the vigilant openmindedness of Ibsen. It must at once greatly deepen the sense of moral responsibility. Before conversion the individual anticipates nothing worse in the way of examination at the judgment bar of his conscience than such questions as, Have you kept the commandments? Have you obeyed the law? Have you attended church regularly? paid your rates and taxes to Caesar? and contributed, in reason, to charitable institutions? It may be hard to do all these things; but it is still harder not to do them, as our ninety-nine moral cowards in the hundred well know. And even a scoundrel can do them all and yet live a worse life than the smuggler or prostitute who must answer No all through the catechism. Substitute for such a technical examination one in which the whole point to be settled is, Guilty or Not Guilty? one in which there is no more and no less respect for virginity than for incontinence, for subordination than for rebellion, for legality than for illegality, for piety than for blasphemy: in short, for the standard qualities than for the standard faults, and immediately, instead of lowering the ethical standard by relaxing the tests of worth, you raise it by increasing their stringency to a point at which no mere Pharisaism or moral cowardice can pass them.

Naturally this does not please the Pharisee. The respectable lady of the strictest Church principles, who has brought up her children with such relentless regard to their ideal morality that if they have any spirit left in them by the time they arrive at years of independence they use their liberty to rush deliriously to the devil: this unimpeachable woman has always felt it unjust that the respect she wins should be accompanied by deep-seated detestation, whilst the latest spiritual heiress of Nell Gwynne, whom no respectable person dare bow to in the street, is a popular idol. The reason is—though the idealist lady does not know it—that Nell Gwynne is a better woman than she; and the abolition of the idealist test which brings her out a worse one, and its replacement by the realist test which would shew the true relation between them, would be a most desirable step forward in public morals, especially as it would act impartially, and set the good side

of the Pharisee above the bad side of the Bohemian as ruthlessly as it would set the good side of the Bohemian above the bad side of the Pharisee.[2] For as long as convention goes counter to reality in these matters, people will be led into Hedda Gabler's error of making an ideal of vice. If we maintain the convention that the distinction between Catherine of Russia and Queen Victoria, between Nell Gwynne and Mrs. Proudie, is the distinction between a bad woman and a good woman, we need not be surprised when those who sympathize with Catherine and Nell conclude that it is better to be a loose woman than a strict one, and go on recklessly to conceive a prejudice against teetotalism and monogamy, and a prepossession in favour of alcoholic excitement and promiscuous amours. Ibsen himself is kinder to the man who has gone his own way as a rake and a drunkard than to the man who is respectable because he dare not be otherwise. We find that the franker and healthier a boy is, the more certain is he to prefer pirates and highwaymen, or Dumas musketeers, to "pillars of society" as his favorite heroes of romance. We have already seen both Ibsenites and anti-Ibsenites who seem to think that the cases of Nora and Mrs. Elvsted are meant to establish a golden rule for women who wish to be "emancipated": the said golden rule being simply, Run away from your husband. But in Ibsen's view of life, that would come under the same condemnation as the ecclesiastical rule, Cleave to your husband until death do you part. Most people know of a case or two in which it would be wise for a wife to follow the example of Nora or even of Mrs. Elvsted. But they must also

---

[2] The warning implied in this sentence is less needed now than it was twenty years ago. The association of Bohemianism with the artistic professions and with revolutionary political views has been weakened by the revolt of the children of the Bohemians against its domestic squalor and social outlawry. Bohemianism is now rather one of the stigmata of the highly conservative "smart sets" of the idle rich than of the studio, the stage, and the Socialist organizations. (1912)

know cases in which the results of such a course would be as tragi-comic as those of Gregers Werle's attempt in *The Wild Duck* to do for the Ekdal household what Lona Hessel did for the Bernick household. What Ibsen insists on is that there is no golden rule; that conduct must justify itself by its effect upon life and not by its conformity to any rule or ideal. And since life consists in the fulfilment of the will, which is constantly growing, and cannot be fulfilled to-day under the conditions which secured its fulfilment yesterday, he claims afresh the old Protestant right of private judgment in questions of conduct as against all institutions, the so-called Protestant Churches themselves included.

Here I must leave the matter, merely reminding those who may think that I have forgotten to reduce Ibsenism to a formula for them, that its quintessence is that there is no formula.

H. L. Mencken

The Technical Quality of the Plays

IBSEN, like Wagner and Manet, has lived down his commentators, and is now ready to be examined and enjoyed for what he actually was, namely, a first-rate journeyman dramatist, perhaps the best that ever lived. Twenty years ago he was hymned and damned as anything and everything else: symbolist, seer, prophet, necromancer, maker of riddles, rabble-rouser, cheap shocker, pornographer, spinner of gossamer nothings. Fools belabored him and fools defended him; he was near to being suffocated and done for in the fog of balderdash. I know of no sure cure for all the sorrows of the world, social, political or aesthetic, that was not credited to him, read into him, forced into his baggage. And I know of no crime against virtue, good order and the revelation of God that he was not accused of. The product of all this pawing and bawling was the Ibsen legend, that fabulous picture of a fabulous monster, half Nietzsche and half Dr. Frank Crane, drenching the world with scandalous platitudes from a watch-tower in the chilblained North. The righteous heard of him with creepy shudders; there was bold talk of denying him the use of the mails; he was the Gog and the Magog, the Heliogabalus, nay the downright Kaiser, of that distant and pious era.

No such Ibsen, of course, ever really existed. The genuine Ibsen was anything but the Anti-Christ thus conjured up by imprudent partisans and terrified opponents. On the contrary, he was a man whose salient quality was precisely his distrust of, and disdain for, any and all such facile heresies; a highly respectable gentleman of the middle class, well-barbered, ease-loving and careful in mind; a very skilful practitioner of a very exacting and lucrative trade; a safe and sane exponent of order, efficiency, honesty and common sense. From end to end of his life there is no record that Ibsen ever wrote a single word or formulated a single idea that might not have been exposed in a newspaper editorial. He believed in all the things that the normal, law-abiding citizen of Christendom believes in, from democracy to romantic love, and from the obligations of duty to the value of virtue, and he always gave them the best of it in his plays. And whenever, mistaking his position, someone charged him with flouting these things or with advocating some notion that stood in opposition to them, he invariably called the plaintiff to book, and denied vehemently that he was guilty, and protested bitterly that it was outrageous to fasten any such wild and naughty stuff upon a reputable man.

Had he been, in truth, the extravagant iconoclast that a misinformed rabbinism tried to make him out, he would have remained, to the end of his career, a mere freak and blank cartridge in the theatre, and of no more influence than such extremists, say, as Max Stirner, Arthur Gobineau and the Marquis de Sade. So long, indeed, as he was generally held to be such an iconoclast, he actually suffered that fate. But when it began to be noticed, first by other dramatists and then by a widening public, that his ideas, after all, were really not extraordinary—that what he said, in the last analysis, was simply what every reasonably intelligent man thought—that his plays, for all their smashing air, were not

Reprinted from *Eleven Plays of Henrik Ibsen*. Published by Random House, Inc., New York [1935]. Reprinted by permission. Editor's title.

actually blows at Christian culture—when this began to be understood, then he began to make his way, and all the serious dramatists of Europe began to imitate him. But they saw him, with their keener professional eyes, more clearly than the early and so absurd Ibsenites had seen him. They saw that he was not a brummagem prophet, but a play-maker of astounding skill—one who had a new and better method to teach them. And so, when they set out to follow him, what they imitated was not the imaginary mystifications that foolish fuglemen had read into his dramas, but his direct and adept manner of clothing simple and even self-evident arguments in unusually lucid and brilliant dramatic forms—in brief, his enormously effective technique as a dramatist. He didn't teach them to think extraordinary thoughts; he taught them to put obvious thoughts into sound plays.

All this must be plain to anyone who goes through his so-called social dramas today, despite the confusing memory of all the gabble that went about in the high days of the Ibsen uproar. What ideas does one actually find in them? Such ideas, first and last, as even a Harvard professor might evolve without bursting his brain—for example, that it is unpleasant and degrading for a wife to be treated as a mere mistress and empty-head; that professional patriots and town boomers are frauds; that success in business usually involves doing things that a self-respecting man hesitates to do; that a woman who continues to cohabit with a syphilitic husband may expect to have defective children; that a joint sorrow tends to dampen passion in husband and wife, and so bring them together upon a more secure basis; that a neurotic and lascivious woman is apt to be horrified when she finds that she is pregnant; that a man of 55 or 60 is an ass to fall in love with a flapper of 17; that the world is barbarously cruel to a women who has violated the Seventh Commandment or a man who has violated the Eighth. If you are discontented with these summaries, then turn to summaries that Ibsen made himself—that is, turn to his notes for his social dramas in his *Nachgelassene Schriften.* Here you will find precisely what he was trying to say. Here you will find, in plain words, the ideas that he started from. They are, without exception, ideas of the utmost simplicity. There is nothing mysterious in them; there is not even anything new in them. Above all, there is no idiotic symbolism in them. They mean just what they say.

As I have said, Ibsen himself was under no delusions about his dramas of ideas. He was a hard-working dramatist and a mere man of sense: he never allowed the grotesque guesses and fantasies of his advocates to corrupt the clarity of his own purpose. Down to the time he lost his mind—he was then at work on *John Gabriel Borkman*—he never wrote a line that had any significance save the obvious one, and he never forgot for an instant that he was writing, not tracts, but stage-plays. When the sentimental German middle classes mistook *A Doll's House* for a revolutionary document against monogamy, and began grouping him with the preachers of free love, he was as indignant as only a respectable family man can be, and even agreed to write a new ending for the play in order to shut off that nonsense. A year later he wrote *Ghosts* to raise a laugh against the alarmed moralists who had swallowed the free lovers' error. The noise of combat continuing, he decided to make an end of it by burlesquing the Ibsenists, and the result was *The Wild Duck,* in which the chief figure is a sort of *reductio ad absurdum* of the modern Drama Leaguer. In *The Master Builder* he took a holiday from social ideas, even the most elemental, and put himself into a play, shedding a salt tear over his lost youth. And in *Hedda Gabler,* as if to confute the Ibsen talmudists forever, he fashioned a thumping drama out of the oldest, shoddiest materials of Sardou, Scribe and Feuillet, nay, Meilhac and Halévy, as if to prove, once and for all time, that he was a dramatist first and last, and not a windy evangelist and reformer, and that he could meet any other dramatist, however skilful, on equal terms, and dispose of him neatly and completely.

Ibsen's chief interest, from the beginning to the end of his career as a dramatist, was not with the propagation of ethical ideas, but with the solution of aesthetic problems. He was, in brief, not a preacher, but an artist, and not the moony artist of popular legend, but the alert and competent artist of fact, intent upon the technical difficulties of his business. He gave infinitely more thought to questions of practical dramaturgy—to getting his characters on and off the stage, to building up climaxes, to calculating effects—than he ever gave to the ideational content of his dramas. Almost any idea was good enough, so long as it could be converted into a conflict, and the conflict could be worked out straightforwardly and effectively. Read his letters and you will find him tremendously concerned, from the start, with technical difficulties and expedients—and never mentioning morals, lesson, symbols and that sort of thing at all. So early as the time he wrote *The League of Youth* you will find him discussing the details of dramatic machinery with Dr. Georg Brandes, and laying stress on the fact, with no little vanity, that he has "accomplished the feat of doing without a single monologue, in fact, without a single aside." A bit later he began developing the stage direction; go through his plays and observe how he gradually increased its importance, until in the end it almost overshadowed the dialogue. And if you would get, in brief, the full measure of his contribution to the art of the drama, give hard study to *A Doll's House*. Here, for the first time, his new technique was in full working. Here he deposed Scribe and company at one blow, and founded an entirely new order of dramaturgy. Other dramatists, long before him, had concocted dramas of ideas—and good ones. The idea in Augier's *La Mariage d'Olympe* was quite as sound and interesting as that in *A Doll's*

House; the idea in Augier's *Les Effrontés* perhaps exceeded it in both ways. But Ibsen got into *A Doll's House* something that Augier and Feuillet and Dumas *fils* and all that crowd of Empire dramatists had never been able to get into their plays, and that was an air of utter and absolute reality, an overwhelming conviction, a complete concealment of the dramatic machinery.

And how did he conceal it? Simply by leaving it out. Scribe had built up an inordinately complex dramaturgy. His plays were elaborate and beautiful mechanisms, but still always mechanisms. He had to sacrifice everything else—reason, probability, human nature—to make the machine run. And Augier, Feuillet and Dumas, better men all, followed docilely in his tracks. They were better observers; they were more keenly interested in the actual life about them; they managed, despite the artificiality of their technique, to get some genuine human beings into their plays. But that technique still hung around their necks; they never quite got rid of it. But Ibsen did. In *A Doll's House* he threw it overboard for all time. Instead of a complicated plot, working beautifully toward a foreordained climax, he presented a few related scenes in the life of a husband and wife. Instead of a finely wrought fabric of suspense and emotion nicely balanced, neatly hanging together, he hit upon an action that was all suspense and all emotion. And instead of carefully calculated explanations, involving the orthodox couriers and prattling chambermaids, he let the story tell itself. The result, as William Archer has said, "was a new order of experience in the theatre." The audience that came to be pleasantly diverted by the old, old tricks found its nerves racked by a glimpse through a terrifying keyhole. This thing was not a stage-play, but a scandal. It didn't caress and soothe; it arrested and shocked. It didn't stay discreetly on the stage; it leaped out over the footlights.

The audience gasped and went out gabbling, and the result was the Ibsen mad-ness, with its twenty years of folderol. But there were dramatists in the house who, with professional eye, saw more clearly what was afoot, and these dramatists, once they could shake off the Scribe tradition, began to imitate Ibsen—Jones and Pinero and later Shaw in England; Hauptmann and Sudermann in Germany; Gorki and many another in Russia; Hervieu, Brieux and their like in France; a swarm of lesser ones in Italy, Scandinavia and Austria. Ibsen, in brief, completely overthrew the well-made play of Scribe, and set up the play that was a direct imitation of reality. He showed that the illusion was not only not helped by the elaborate machinery of Scribe, but that it was actually hindered— that the way to sure and tremendous effects was by the route of simplicity, naturalness, ingenuousness. In *A Doll's House* he abandoned all of the old tricks save two or three; in *Ghosts* he made away with the rest of them, and even managed to do without a plot; by the time he got to *Little Eyolf* there was nothing left of the traditional dramaturgy save the act divisions. It was not, of course, an easy reform to put through. The habits of mind of audiences had to be changed; the lunacies of the Ibsenites had to be lived down, and the moral ire of the anti-Ibsenites; above all, the actors of the time had to be untaught all that they knew about acting, and taught a lot of new things that violated their vanity and hurt their business. But Ibsen's notions had logic behind them, and they had the force of novelty, and there was in them a new and superior opportunity for the dramatist who really had something to say, and so, in the end, they triumphed in the world. Today the methods of Scribe are so archaic that they excite laughter; only the Broadhursts and Kleins of Broadway stoop to them. If an intelligent dramatist were to expose a play built upon the plans of *Verre d'Eau* or *Adrienne Lecouvreur,* even the newspaper critics would laugh at him. All that sort of thing now belongs to archeology.

But Ibsen, as I have said, was a dramatist first and last, and not a tin-pot agitator and messiah. He depicted the life of his time and he made use of the ideas of his time; he had no desire to change those ideas, nor even, in the main, to criticise them. "A dramatist's business," he used to say, "is not to answer questions, but merely to ask them." He asked a question in *A Doll's House.* He asked another, ironically, in *Ghosts.* He asked others in *The Lady from the Sea, The Wild Duck* and *Little Eyolf.* In *The Master Builder,* rising, so to speak, to a question of personal privilege, he abandoned his habit and ventured upon a half-answer. But is there any answer in *Hedda Gabler?* Surely not. The play is still chewed and belabored by advocates of this answer or that; the very lack of agreement shows the dramatist's neutrality. "It was not my desire," he once said, "to deal in this play with so-called problems. What I wanted to do was to depict human beings, human emotions, and human destinies, upon a groundwork of certain of the social conditions and principles of the present day." That is to say, here is your state of society, here is your woman, here is what she does—what do you think of it? So, again, in *Pillars of Society.* Here is your society, here are your pillars, here are their rascalities—what have you to say of it? Joseph Conrad, another great artist, once put the thing admirably. "My task which I am trying to achieve," he said, "is, by the power of the written word, to make you hear, to make you feel—it is, before all, to make you *see.* That—and no more, and it is everything."

Eric Bentley

Ibsen, Pro and Con

IT MUST have been a pleasure to welcome Ibsen with open arms when all one's primmer relatives were shaking their fists at him, but the great days of Ibsenism are past. Today the mention of the Norwegian's name elicits, in many quarters, a certain feeling of tedium. After all, the Ibsenites won all too complete a victory: their man was accepted into the dull ranks of fame; he became an academic figure.

A supremely great writer like Shakespeare can survive such acceptance—with whatever wear and tear. It is harder for a genius of the second rank; the livelier reader is apt to think Ibsen well deserves his dim respectability. It would be better if he belonged to the third rank and did not raise such high expectations! Ibsen so often leads us to expect the highest things that we are disturbed when he falls short. He is an author we worry about. From time to time we wonder—as we do not wonder about Shakespeare: is he really good or have we been imposed upon?

If we are to return to him, if we are to read and see him freshly, it cannot be by ignoring such worries. Before hearing a spokesman *for* Ibsen, let us hear a devil's advocate voice our misgivings.

CON

When we open our Ibsen we enter an unconvincing world: a world created by bad prose, clumsy dramatic structures, and stale ideas. Since you will tell me that the bad prose is the work of his translators, I will concentrate on the structures and the ideas.

How could H. L. Mencken feel that Ibsen abolished the artificial "well-made play" and just let the facts "tell themselves"? Hadn't he read *Ghosts?* At the end of Act II Mrs. Alving's story is just "telling itself" when—lest it all come blurting out before our evening at the theater is done—Ibsen has a sanatorium catch fire. This is disastrously clumsy dramatic construction. The craftsman's machinery overwhelms the poet's vision.

Is not the same true of *A Doll's House?* Krogstad, for example, is a mere pawn of the plot. When convenient to Ibsen, he is a blackmailer. When inconvenient, he is converted. Ibsen the craftsman is busy constructing relationships between two couples —Torvald and Nora, Krogstad and Mrs. Linde. The parallels and contrasts must work out right, even if the characterization is impaired.

Dr. Rank is not the pawn of the plot— he is not even necessary to it—but he is the pawn of an idea. When Ibsen wants to bring the theme of hereditary disease and death before us he has only to write "Enter Dr. Rank." You will tell me that Dr. Rank is a symbolic character, and that symbolism is one of the elements in the total structure of an Ibsen play. The trouble is that Ibsen's symbolism is so portentous—what with the sanatorium burning to show us that the Alvings are burning and Rank dropping his black cross in the letter box to show us that death is in the background!

In *An Enemy of the People, A Doll's House,* and *Ghosts* the symbolism is obvious to the point of being tiresome; in *The Master Builder* it is obscure to the point of being confused. I don't mean that the reader of *The Master Builder* has nothing to hold on to. Every little Freudian nowadays knows what to say about the towers and Solness's inability to climb them. Biographers are at hand to explain that Ibsen was tired of writing "social" plays, as Solness was tired of building homes for human beings. What then? The play as a whole is bewildering. Whatever human reality Ibsen may have meant to show us is hidden behind a wilderness of trolls, birds of prey, helpers and servers, devils (good and bad, blond and brunette), fairy kingdoms and castles in the air. The symbolism proliferates. The total result is a mess.

Then there are the ideas, Ibsen's famous ideas: there should be votes for women; women's rights are equal to men's; hereditary syphilis is a bad thing; mercy killing is sometimes justified; keep germs out of the bath-water; don't be jealous of the younger generation, and so forth. If my phrasing is flippant, blame Ibsen, whose presentation of problems is always either ridiculous or vague: the greatest actress who ever played Mrs. Alving—Eleanora Duse—admitted as much. What, for instance, lies behind the nebulous Victorian terms in which Mrs. Alving's life with her husband is dressed? As a critic has already asked: did she never enjoy it when she went to bed with him? Not the least little bit? Again, if my phrasing is flippant, Ibsen asks for it: his kind of drama raises such questions without supplying the answers. Consequently it is impossible to grasp his characters in the way he seems to want you to grasp them.

Oswald in Paris is as cloudy a figure as his mother in his father's bedroom. A matter we should be clear about is whether his disease *must* have come from his father or whether he could not have contracted syphilis from his own sexual activities. At one moment he seems to say "No" to the latter question. "I have never lived recklessly in any sense. . . . I have never done that"; but soon after he says: "I ought to have had nothing to do with the joyous happy life I had lived with my comrades. It had been too much for my strength. So it was my own fault. . . . My whole life incurably ruined—just because of my own imprudence." This last speech is not conclusive, but that is precisely the trouble: conclusiveness is called for. Perhaps one does not care what the doctors say of Oswald's collapse in Act III. Perhaps one can forgive Ibsen for his unscrupulously melodramatic timing of the collapse. But there are many details that could be clear and aren't. For example: Oswald argues that the Parisian artists prefer living unmarried with their children's mothers because it is cheaper. But is it?

A picture composed of such unclear details can only come together in our minds as a fog. Is any clear attitude defined to the famous "modern ideas" to be found in the play? And how far do they go? One assumes that the books Mrs. Alving reads— and which Ibsen does not name—are typical of nineteenth-century liberalism. Yet in one curious passage she goes far beyond ordinary enlightenment into the assumption that we should accept even incest. Ibsen being Ibsen, the suggestion is not clarified.

If *Ghosts* is not exactly a "drama of ideas" it will be better to instance a play that *is—An Enemy of the People*. Dr. Stockman expects his fellow townsmen to accept the truth, however they may be affected by it. He finds, however, that people refuse to accept a truth if it interferes with their interests, that the liberal opposition goes along with the interested minority, and that the masses soon follow suit. He therefore decides—in Act IV—that he is against majority rule.

This is straightforward, if not profound. It is in the fifth act that Ibsen proves himself a muddlehead. Vehement as Stockman is in rejecting common folk as "curs," he firmly intends to educate them. He will begin by educating his own boys and a handful of street urchins. He will train the curs to the point where they can drive out the wolves. "You shan't learn a blessed thing . . . but I will make liberal-minded and high-minded men out of you." That is to say: "The voice of the people is not the voice of God till the people has been educated by me."

Even if we share Stockman's high opinion of himself we must ask how he can secure his position as an educator in a country where the majority are curs. Even in a more fortunate land how can we make the philosopher a king? *An Enemy of the People* is a manifesto for the petty bourgeois, the petty snob, the petty intellectual. The masses are ignorant, you are cultured, therefore you disbelieve in democracy, you believe in culture. What of it? You haven't made it clear how you can attain power. In any case, as a leader you are self-appointed, and that is a game many can play at: *anyone* can declare himself a leader, cultured or otherwise.

Are you going to say that Stockman is not Ibsen? There is precious little evidence within the play that the latter is critical of his creation. The whole play breathes the perennial self-complacency of the arrogant idealist—from the Pharisee of the first century to the Communist intellectual of today. That Ibsen felt compelled to show the other side of the medal in *The Wild Duck* can hardly comfort the critic of *An Enemy of the People*. It takes more than two one-sided plays to make a single two-sided masterpiece. And *An Enemy* is one-sided, a play of moral blacks and whites. To read it as a subtle study in self-righteousness, like *Le Misanthrope*, would be to conceive another play. Stockman is an Alceste taken pretty much at his own valuation.

As a piece of thinking, *An Enemy of the People* is too superficial to be instructive. As a piece of art, it is too feeble to be influential. In 1950 it would be as easy as it is wise to let Ibsen rest in peace.

PRO

I do not find either Ibsen's ideas or his forms as disastrously dated as you assume.

Let me begin where you left off—with the ideas. Are even the ones you mentioned really outmoded? I believe they only *sound* so. "Women's rights," for example. The phrase itself is not in use today—but for that matter it isn't used in *A Doll's House*. The problem as to what women's rights *are* is still real enough. The world is still a man's world, and if the status of women has been raised, it is still a secondary and an awkward status. In 1950 there are still many "doll's houses." As for *Ghosts*, hereditary disease is still with us, mercy killing is still a controversial question. And as for *The Master Builder*, the conflict of the generations is as real as ever.

Even the play you take as the very type of outmoded "drama of ideas"—*An Enemy of the People*—is neither as transparent nor as wrong as you make it appear. Certainly Stockman's philosophy is supererogatory in a country like Germany, where too many people already share it. In America it might be a salutary challenge. The American philosophy of the common man needs constant criticism if it is to be preserved from demagogic sentimentality. The idealism of many people today begins in self-contempt and functions as a flight from the self; Stockman, whatever his failings, knew that morality must start from self-respect. You seem to consider the Ibsen who wrote *An Enemy* facile, trivial, journalistic. Just compare the portrait of a Norwegian community given in Steinbeck's *The Moon Is Down*. There can be no doubt who gives the keener, stricter, more deeply pondered view.

But these are side issues. More essential is the fact that in discussing Ibsen's ideas you mentioned only those that jump to the eyes, the famous "social" ideas that scandalized conservative Victorians and delighted the Ibsenite rebels. Led astray, perhaps, by some of the latter, you, too, seem to expect Ibsen to be primarily a brain. Perhaps you demand that his ideas be brilliant and original and that he juggle them with the skill of a logician. I, on the other hand, shall argue that you have failed to notice what are the most active ideas in Ibsen's plays and that you are therefore unable to see what use he put them to.

What ideas are most active in *Ghosts?* Surely not those you have mentioned. Behind the question of mercy killing is the question of "modern ideas" generally—as against the "established ideas" of Pastor Manders. To perpetrate a mercy killing, a person would have to be emancipated entirely from established ideas. Ibsen brings the matter up, one might almost say, to show that Mrs. Alving is *not* so emancipated. He is less interested in "modern ideas" themselves than in certain ideas that go behind them. In Ibsen one must always look for the idea behind the idea.

Ibsen did not by any means stop with the conflict of modern and established ideas. His special achievement is the depth and body he gives to each of these philosophies as it exists in people's lives. He does this not as an agile arguer but as a poet with a country, a people, a tradition behind him. Abstract ideas take concrete form through (for example) his use of folk imagery. Established ideas he sees as "ghosts," as "the spirits of the dead" of popular belief; and if Mrs. Alving strives after modernity, she does so, not as the "new woman" of the Paris boulevards, but as a daughter of the Vikings. Below the surface of "modern," "Christian" civilization Ibsen finds "primitive," "pagan" forces. It is to Norse paganism he looks alike for images of evil and for images of human dignity—here, rather than in those modern books which, so you insinuate, he doesn't even know the titles of. His superior people are to be understood as Vikings *manqués.* Mrs. Alving thinks she ought, like some rash pagan, to countenance incest, but she can't bring herself to do so. The great surprise of *A Doll's House* is our discovery of a Viking spirit in Torvald's little squirrel. Halvard Solness is a man who *had been* a Viking—ten years earlier. If you will agree to call *this* Ibsen's "idea," you will not find *The Master Builder* so bewildering.

Compared with Mrs. Alving, Solness is a strong man. But if the weaker Ibsen characters are held back by "the spirits of the dead," the stronger are goaded on by "the trolls of the mountain." [1] Early in *A Doll's House* Nora is characterized as a "mad creature," and later, when she dances the tarantella, the "troll in her" takes over. In *The Master Builder* the trolls come for Solness in the person of Hilda Wangel—or that part of her which is a bird of prey. They goad him into attempting the impossible. Being a Viking no longer, he cannot climb as high as he builds. He falls to his death.

I am not offering Norse mythology as a magic key to Ibsen. My point is simply that one can always look in Ibsen for something beyond the clichés of the problem drama. Take the most famous problem play of them all. *A Doll's House* seems to you to be about votes for women, a topic that does not come up in the play at all. What does come up is the matter of woman's place in a man's world, a much larger topic that still bristles with interest today. It even seems to me that Ibsen pushes his investigation toward a further and even deeper subject, the tyranny of one human being over another; in this respect the play would be just as valid were Torvald the wife and Nora the husband.

Reread the opening pages of *A Doll's House.* Since the text is familiar, you are not just picking up the facts of the story; you are noticing the terms in which Ibsen presents his subject. No words are lost. Nora's tipping the porter a shilling instead of sixpence not only gives us her character

[1] "The troll is not a puck or a goblin; he is truly diabolic. Although the old stories spoke of monstrous three-headed trolls, the troll may look much like a human being; only a little stocky, a little malformed. A troll is humanity minus the specifically human qualities; at once a hideous parody of man and yet only the isolation of his worst potentialities. . . . The troll is the animal version of man, the alternative to man: he is also what man fears he may become."—*Ibsen the Norwegian,* by M. C. Bradbrook.

but establishes money as one of the topics of the play. The borrowing of money—which lies at the heart of the action—is mentioned soon and is opposed to the possibility of freedom and beauty. The making of lots of money is seen by Torvald and Nora as a basis for security, a life free from care; yet when we meet someone who actually married for money, we have a sense of foreboding. . . . The references to money all lead into the play—taken as a play—and culminate in Nora's "Torvald, this is a settling of accounts." You must, after all, regard *A Doll's House* as drama even when your topic is the ideas. The ideas thread their way in and out, as it were, as themes. The theme of money, for example. Money is at the root of so much that happens in *A Doll's House*. Ibsen has, if you like, an "idea" about money. He doesn't philosophize about it. He lets it find expression through the action and the characters.

You managed to speak of four Ibsen plays without noticing an "idea" common to them all—an idea about disease. For Ibsen, disease is not only one of the facts of life in general but a symbol of modern life in particular. You doubtless recall Solness's sickly conscience, Oswald's rotting body and mind, and you mentioned Dr. Rank. Don't you find Ibsen adroit when he introduces the disease theme in Rank's opening discussion of Krogstad, at once tranfers it from the physical to the moral sphere, then applies it to society at large?

Admittedly a formula such as "Modern life—a disease" is little or nothing in itself. Ibsen makes dramatic use of it. He sets it in motion. He makes it grow. In *An Enemy of the People*, Act II, Hovstad explains that the morass which the town is built on is not physical but moral. In Act III Stockman realizes that "it is the whole of our social life that we have got to purify and disinfect." The idea gathers momentum and has, as it were, a climax, along with the rest of the play's action, in Act IV. "It is not they who are most instrumental in poisoning the sources of our moral life and infecting the

ground on which we stand . . . it is the masses, the majority."

When I turn your attention from the ideas themselves to Ibsen's use of them, I don't mean Ibsen didn't take ideas seriously, but that his seriousness about them and the force of the ideas themselves come out more in the way he has them operate than in anything he explicitly says. His criticism of life is made less in general formulations than in ironical juxtaposition of the facts. It has often been shown that Ibsen interweaves, intertwines, interlocks his materials. His dialogue is all implication, all cross-reference. This is his famous method.[2] It is important to see in it, not a system of meaningless theatrical trickery, but an exquisitely apt expression of Ibsen's awareness.

I grant you that when he became a virtuoso Ibsen succumbed to some of the virtuoso's temptations. His technique is sometimes obtrusive, and often the lines creak and groan beneath the load of double, treble, and quadruple significance. I only ask you not, in protesting against the defect, to forget the quality. As to the overall structure of an Ibsen play,[3] for example, it is misleading to observe that Ibsen used a highly artificial, not to say sensational, pattern borrowed from the Parisian hacks and handed back to them afterward, if we do not add that this pattern exactly suited Ibsen's deeper purpose. For the hacks, it was a toy—and thus an end in itself, though, by definition, a childish one. For Ibsen, it was the instrument of a vision.

Historians of the drama explain that Ibsen took over from the Parisian hacks the story of the long-buried secret that eventually leaks out with sensational results. They sometimes forget to add that Ibsen saw life itself as a placid surface through which, from time to time, what seemed dead

[2] How the method works out in *Ghosts* is demonstrated in *The Play: A Critical Anthology*, edited by Eric Bentley.
[3] The best descriptions are still to be found in *Playmaking*, by William Archer.

and buried will break—a present into which the "vanished" past returns. Perhaps they are indifferent to the meaning of all this— that there is moral continuity between past and present, that concealment (repression, hypocrisy) is the enemy, openness (candor, light, truth) the one thing necessary. If so, they miss the point of Ibsen's famous expositions: as pure technique they would be barren exercises; what justifies them is the way they render the interaction of past and present. The curtain goes up ten years after Nora and Mrs. Linde last met, ten years after the death of Alving, ten years after the meeting of Solness and Hilda. Ibsen confronts one decade in his people's lives with another. The plot-pattern gives exact expression alike to his direct vision of life and to his subsequent interpretation of it.

To your contention that Ibsen's plots ride him, rather than he them, I reply that I could give more examples of the contrary. One is to be found at the end of *A Doll's House*. If the plot dominated the play, the culminating-point would be Torvald's discovery of Nora's secret. Ibsen's achievement is to have subordinated this external event to Nora's inner realization that Torvald is incapable of nobly taking the blame for what she has done. The dramatically active question of the last act is whether the "wonderful thing" will happen or not. The scene in which Nora realizes that it won't is one of the great scenes in modern drama not only in precipitating some mordant speeches—"It is a thing hundreds of thousands of women have done"— but in occasioning a magnificently dramatic silence—that of Nora gradually realizing that Torvald is a broken reed. A few words escape her, but the process of realization is silent.

I should not leave the subject of Ibsen's dramatic art without a word on his mastery of the theatrical occasion. He isn't writing novels in dialogue form; he is writing for actors before the eyes of an audience. I suspect that, like so many moderns, you are primarily a novel-reader who resents not finding in Ibsen all that he finds in fiction. If you think Ibsen lacks the skills of Henry James you should recognize that he has others which James lacks, the skills of the theater rather than of the book. If of course you simply prefer the novel to the drama, there is no more to be said: you will naturally prefer James's gradual, word-by-word definition of his subject to Ibsen's definition by upheaval. If, on the other hand, you can respect the theatrical medium, you will appreciate the effect on the spectator of, say, Hilda Wangel's first irruption onto the stage with her alpenstock and knapsack, Mrs. Alving's "registering" the offstage laughter of Regina and Oswald, Nora's suddenly appearing in her street clothes. . . . Such things are addressed to the eyes of an audience, not to the imagination of a solitary reader.

"Ibsen and the Actor" is a huge topic, for not only did he write for actors (like every other playwright); he gave the actor something essentially new and asked him for something essentially new in return: a new style. He brought to completion a development in the art of acting that had been under way for centuries—the humanizing of the actor, the conversion of a hierophant into a man. In Ibsen that part of man which the ancient mime kept covered—the face—is the very center of the performance. The individual spirit looks out of the eyes and shapes its thoughts with the lips.

But this is, no doubt, too special a subject for your taste. Let me try to sum up my rejoinder to your protest. I think you have too limited a conception of the way in which an artist teaches. Ibsen, for example, is not—or not in the first instance—providing a list of recommended virtues and deplored vices. In this regard he is singularly modest. He has written only a preface to morals. He asks for that degree of honor, honesty, integrity, truth, what you will, which is needed before a moral life can exist. We have seen that he tells over and again the story of the disastrous effects of concealment and burial. He is asking us, not necessarily to be saints and heroes, but at least to stand upright, at least—like Goethe's Faust—to assume responsibilities and make ethical distinctions, to be authentic human beings. Ibsen does not have his people follow the track of any particular virtue. He shows Nora and Mrs. Alving trying to discover themselves and reach the threshold of morality, the point where virtues—and, of course, vices—begin. So much of our life is too meaningless or too infantile even to be called vicious.

This criticism of life places Ibsen, not in the piddling tradition of the problem play, but at the very heart of our contemporary discussion of ourselves. He is one of the great modern writers. Like most of the others he has presented modern life to us in the form of fable, parable, myth; and once you realize that his medium was theater and not the book, you will not find his fables inferior to those of other masters. Ibsen is a poet. Although he gave up verse, he managed to enrich and intensify his work by so many other means that the verse plays of the best poets since his time— T. S. Eliot's, for example—seem dilute and "unpoetic" by comparison.

Forty years ago a decadent poet—who evidently despised Ibsen's dialogue in general—could refer to Hilda Wangel's "harps in the air" as a feeble, if praiseworthy, attempt at lyricism. Strange that he hadn't more feeling for the *context* of Hilda's phrase, for that dry, prose understatement against which "harps in the air" comes as a contrast, an intentionally brief glimpse of another order of experience! I do not mean to interpret the dry, prose understatement as a merely negative factor. A generation that has read Gertrude Stein and Ernest Hemingway knows better than that. Ibsen is a great realist, not least in his imaginative use of unimaginative language.

Of recent years those of us who admire Ibsen's "poetry" have probably understressed his "realism." It is a pity the two words are used antithetically. Ibsen was a great poet—that is, he had a great imagina-

tion that found its outlet in words—but it would be foolish to try to detach him from the realist movement. He quite consciously channeled his energies into it. It was as a realist that he made his first impact, and, in closing my counterstatement, I shall maintain that it is partly as a realist that he must still make his impact today.

In refusing to squeeze Ibsen into the narrow category of the problem play we need not neglect to view him historically. There is a pedantry of historical scholarship that reduces artists to statistics and vaguely defined abstractions, but there is also history itself—man and all his works in the flux of time. I should prefer to see *any* artist in this context rather than in context of timeless forms and timeless ideas— and Ibsen above all. For, however we stress his artistry and the breadth of his mind, he was a man up to the neck in his time. We find him relevant today partly because we have still not put his time behind us, partly because the artists who become permanent are precisely those who grasp the ephemeral most firmly and not those whose eyes are fixed upon eternity.

A more historical view of Ibsen will keep us from exaggerating the "other-worldliness" of a play like—to come back to your bugbear—*The Master Builder*. For, once we realize that Ibsen was not obsessed with syphilis and votes for women, there is a danger of our locating his interest only in the deepest recesses of the individual consciousness. This would be to consider him just as narrow a specialist—only at the other extreme. The glory of Ibsen is that he refused to make certain fatal separations. He refused (for example) to separate the individual from the collective, the personal from the social.

Halvard Solness is seen in both aspects. There is Solness the individual artist: *the symbolism of the play drives inward,* to the rich inner life of the man. There is also Solness the builder of actual houses: I should not be so much inclined as I once was to regard him as a mere front for the more spiritual figure. As Miss Bradbrook says: "Solness belonged to a class which transformed Norway. The replacing of the old wooden houses . . . by modern buildings effected a domestic revolution." *The realism of the play drives outward*, to the rich outer life of the man. If the symbolism and the realism of *The Master Builder* are imperfectly fused—and that may be the source of your difficulty with the play—one realizes that Ibsen could have "perfected" his work by simplifying his problem, by writing a narrowly "symbolic" or a narrowly "realist" play. Surely one prefers a heroic failure.

Not that the word *failure* applies to Ibsen's work as a whole. Artistic failures seldom outlive the artist, yet, a hundred years since Ibsen's first play was written, his words sting and burn, if we let them, as fiercely as ever. No playwright has managed to project into his scenes more of the pressure of modern life, its special anxiety, strain, and stress. The life of our times courses through his plays in a torrent. And if we are a little more conscious than our grandparents were of the care with which Ibsen controlled the flood—his mastery of form—we must still begin where they began—with shock, with enthrallment, with illumination, as Ibsen's world, which is so large a sector of the modern world, social and personal, outer and inner, unfolds before us.

James Walter McFarlane

Revaluations of Ibsen

THE official histories of the original Ibsenite campaign rightly pay close attention to the generalship of Shaw. From our present standpoint in time, one can delight in the vigour of his *Quintessence of Ibsenism,* in the thrustful aggressiveness of his defence, in the brilliant intuition that informed him of the weaknesses in the opposition and his cruel probing of them; but many are now ready to admit that his brilliance in this respect was a tactician's brilliance and that his strategy was misconceived. He elected, as is well known, to join the battle on the grounds that the plays are first and foremost the embodiment of a lesson, illustrations of a thesis, exercises in moral persuasion; he shared Archer's concern for the plays as messages rather than imaginative creations, and even his assessment of Ibsen's technical achievement—the novelty of which he ascribed to the introduction of "the discussion"—rests on this assumption. But the suspicion grew with time that this had been a false appreciation of what was vital to defend. What happened if one persisted in holding to Shavian criteria is shown very clearly in Spengler's *Decline of the West* which began to appear in 1923. There Spengler trod the path of Shavian Ibsenism to its terminus, finally arriving at the conclusion that Ibsen would have to be banished to the lumber room, to be taken out and dusted down for the benefit of accredited researchers only. Spengler was another of those who saw the drama of the late nineteenth century primarily as a medium for agitation and debate. He placed Ibsen in a cyclic phase that began with

Schopenhauer and ended with Shaw, that included the names of Proudhon and Comte, Hebbel and Feuerbach, Marx and Engles, Wagner and Nietzsche, Darwin and John Stuart Mill, the creed of which he defined as "ethical socialism." As for the plays themselves, he considered they were so tied to their own age that they would never be able to claim the attention of later generations; their merits, such as they were, were historical rather than intrinsic. By 1950, asserted Spengler confidently, Ibsen will be quite dead.

But although the ideas of Shavian Ibsenism are nowadays generally discredited, its influence on some Ibsen criticism is still potent. Few are any longer misled into it but many are still misled by it, provoked by it into views that are different but equally unacceptable. One imagines the argument going something like this: Ibsen is after all, on all the evidence, not dead but on the contrary very much alive; yet the things he wrote about, the themes, the ideas, the content of the works, no longer seem to concern us very closely; therefore surely his continued vitality can only be ascribed to his technique. It is not what he said, seemingly, but the way he said it. What indeed, it was once asked by H. L. Mencken, are those once famous ideas?

That it is unpleasant and degrading for a wife to be treated as a mere mistress and empty-head; that professional patriots . . . are frauds; that success in business usually involves doing things that a self-respecting man hesitates to do; that a woman who continues to cohabit with a syphilitic husband may expect to have defective children;

From *Ibsen and the Temper of Norwegian Literature*, Oxford University Press, London and New York, 1960. Reprinted by permission.

. . . that a neurotic and lascivious woman is apt to be horrified when she finds that she is pregnant; . . . that the world is barbarously cruel to a woman who has violated the Seventh Commandment or a man who has violated the Eighth.

Such remarks, which are of course meant to be in defence of Ibsen, claim a timelessness for his ideas only by insisting that they are unremarkable. The ideas are considered as neither adding to nor detracting from the real merit of the plays as honest, workmanlike, journeyman drama. The consequence is that Ibsen has often found himself in post-Shavian criticism taken out of the company of Schopenhauer, Darwin and Nietzsche and associated rather with Scribe and Augier and Feuillet and Dumas *fils* and the tradition of the *pièce bien faite;* he is respected as one who found a successful solution to certain technical problems of dramatic composition.

It is the swing of the pendulum. Whereas the generation of Holbrook Jackson admired Ibsen as a man "whose method of criticizing conventional morals by means of drama had a profound effect upon thinking people," the present generation is inclined rather to echo the words of the Angus Wilson character in *Hemlock and After,* who says: "I admire Ibsen's stagecraft, but I find it more and more difficult to sit through hours of life in the raw." His moral stock has slumped, but this has been balanced by the appreciation in the value attached to his craftsmanship; he maintains his position, it seems, although no longer as a leader of opinion but rather as a technician of the highest order. And a new orthodoxy bemoans the fact that such a talented writer lavished his gifts on such sadly perishable material.

Yet even Shaw, in the most confidently assertive book ever written about Ibsen, disarmingly admitted the folly of making confident assertion: "When you have called Mrs. Alving an emancipated woman or an unprincipled one, Alving a debauchee or a victim of society, Nora a fearless and noble-

hearted woman or a shocking little liar and an unnatural mother, Helmer, a selfish hound or a model husband and father, according to your bias, you have said something which is at once true and false, and in both cases perfectly idle." This is no less true of the conflicting things that have been said about Ibsen himself; and it echoes a phrase from his own *Emperor and Galilean* first isolated and applied to Ibsen by one of his contemporaries in 1873 and equally valid today: "What he is, that he is not, and what he is not, that he is"—a phrase of which the critical literature on Ibsen is in its totality an enactment. The first denials came with what the Ibsenites in their day said to those who felt that they knew only too well what Ibsen was; and having established to their own satisfaction what Ibsen was, were themselves in turn rebuked in the same terms. The landscape of his authorship, once mapped by them as a high central plateau of problematic realism, a region peopled with pillars of society and enemies of the people and ghosts, approached through the bewildering thickets of *Brand* and *Peer Gynt* and falling away "down among the dead men"—this landscape in more recent and more audacious reports is seen as one having as its main feature a triumphantly flowing poetic inspiration, moving in subterranean passages in mid-career, but emerging with enhanced power and sweep in its later reaches.

It becomes increasingly obvious that his genius is of a kind that demands a ceaseless, Forth Bridge-like surveillance, of which it is then meaningless to ask if it is complete but only what point it has reached: whether it is for the moment looking to the "problems" or to the "poetic vision"; whether it is concerned with the investigation of "real people in real situations" or of certain themes, in the enunciation of which the characters are rather the central elements. Whether one calls his dramas the encoded abuse of a fugitive from humiliation, or the occasions for release of private passion, or the night thoughts of one who feared the light, or an audacious and defiant minority report on life; whether one interprets them as the fruits of a mind subtly elated by a sense of secret power or nagged by the possibility that on Sirius two and two might make five; whether one stamps them as visionary or inquisitorial, gnomic or punitive, venomous or introspective—the result is to draw too particular a distinction, is to make assertions that are all equally true, equally false, equally idle.

One thing inevitably emerges from any closer study of Ibsen, something rather unsettling to critical orthodoxy; and this is the realization that he does not seem to react very satisfactorily to any of the standard laboratory tests of criticism; further, that any account of his work that limits itself to what is positive and obtrusive in it seems destined to end in triteness; or else—something which is strange and astonishing in this seemingly so straightforward and uncomplicated author—it turns out that any generalization once made seems to demand reservation and qualification so drastic that the end result is a little short of flat contradiction. Considerations of this kind lend significance to that other expression of admiration of the 1890s, less strident than the official Ibsenism, less partisan, less conspicuous but more durable and one suspects more influential in a rather indirect way—an admiration of which the defining figure is Henry James. To his friend Elizabeth Robins, one of the greatest Ibsen actresses of the decade, he once wrote: "What an old boy is our Northern Henry. He is too delightful—an old darling." What Ibsen might have meant to James personally is suggested by the entry in his Notebooks for 21 December 1896:

I realize—none too soon—that the *scenic* method is my absolute, my imperative, my *only* salvation. The march of an action is the only thing for me to, more and more, attach myself to: it is the only thing that really, for *me*, at least, will *produire* L'ŒUVRE, and L'ŒUVRE is, before God, what

I am going in for. Well, the scenic scheme is the only one *I* can trust, with my tendencies, to stick to the march of an action. How reading Ibsen's splendid John Gabriel a day or two ago (in proof) brought that, FINALLY AND FOREVER, home to me!

James's rather ambivalent admiration for Ibsen as it found expression in certain articles of his—one in June 1891 for the *New Review* on *Hedda Gabler* and another for the *Pall Mall Gazette* in February 1893 on *The Master Builder*, together with two shorter pieces from January and February 1897 in *Harper's Weekly* on *Little Eyolf* and *John Gabriel Borkman*—is generally indifferent to those aspects of the dramas his contemporaries considered most worthy of remark; and it is also obvious that whilst he was impressed by Ibsen's technical mastery, it was not to this exclusively that he looked. There was, however, one thing that quite evidently bewildered him; commenting on what he called Ibsen's "irritating, his bewildering incongruities," he went on: "He is nothing as a literary personality if not positive; and yet there are moments when his great gift seems made up of negatives, or at any rate when the total seems a contradiction of each of the parts." There is reinforcement for this idea also in the words of one of Ibsen's more recent critics, Miss M. C. Bradbrook, who when considering *The Wild Duck* writes: "One day it will be read as a tragedy, the next as the harshest irony; parts of it are clumsy. . . . So searching and yet so delicate is the touch that these flaws and vagaries seem in themselves to strengthen the work."

Both these expressions of view—that a positive is in part made up of negatives, that weaknesses contribute to strength—seem to put certain qualities in Ibsen in an entirely new light. An absence of humour, an absence of free imagination, an absence of glamour, an absence of what is loosely called "style" even, add up to nothing; but in the case of Ibsen they seem to multiply up to what has very suitably been called his "spell." It seems that you cannot mark him independently on, say, content and style with any hope that a conflation of the two assessments will give any adequate index of his achievement. The constituent elements in his drama are not items in a ledger but factors in a product; his technical skill not an additive but rather an exponent in the algebraic sense, his dramas an exponential series in which the plus and minus quantities function in a way altogether different from those that figure in an accountant's statement of profit and loss. One is encouraged to look at the dramas again, to look not at what is positive and obtrusive but at what is (so to speak) conspicuously unobtrusive and even assertively negative. One asks oneself whether this is the occasion to remember the positive significance of the nil return. Should one approach Ibsen as an occasion not for counting the heads but for calling the roll, where it is not the crude total that signifies but rather the meaningful silences and the absence of response? Always remembering, however, that those who seem to be playing truant may all the time be hiding behind the what-not or under the horse-hair sofa.

In the first place there are a number of things that are there but do not show. This is partly the case with his alleged lack of humour. There *is* humour there of a kind and there in abundance, but it is the solitary, unshared, suppressed laughter behind a desperately straight face; there is the tight-lipped fun that he made of contemporary Norwegian society, there is the encoded satire that he aimed at some of his more eminent contemporaries, a code which a study of the draft manuscripts, the letters and the life of the author help to crack; and not least there is the wry ironic detachment with which he turned many a private hurt into a public show. Nor is it so very different with his alleged lack of poetry or imaginative inventiveness. So often one hears the reproach that he is prosaic, uncompromisingly realistic, inveterately observed— a reproach that admittedly sees (say) *Pil-*

lars of Society or *An Enemy of the People* or *Ghosts* as the purest and most characteristic expression of Ibsen's genius, and which is made only after uneasy glances over the shoulder at the luxuriant fantasy of *Peer Gynt*. In the matter of poetic content, one is once again dealing not with some innate deficiency, not with some lack of aptitude, but with a deliberate act of suppression or concealment. In middle life, after the completion of *Brand* and *Peer Gynt*, Ibsen took his resolve to renounce poetry in all its more extravagant or self-conscious forms, to avoid metre, to speak in the language of men talking to men; it was, as it were, the Preface to the *Lyrical Ballads* screwed up another notch. But the poetic vision was not so easily denied; the consequence was a poetry not of a surface beauty but of inner strength, not of fleshy contour but of bony structure, of controlled organization without any concession to prettiness or adornment, and as such it is something surprisingly modern in its assumptions about poetic communication.

As an architect of drama, Ibsen built with the materials of his age; he displays to view a great deal of grey, massive, solid masonry; but at the same time he appears to be doing astonishing things with his conventional material, to be reaching heights of sublime humdrum, to be performing abnormal feats of normality, to be operating within a style of extravagant sobriety. At times his drama seems tremendously firm and monumental, at other times recklessly audacious and top-heavy; it is only on closer inspection, when one has worked out the hidden architecture, that one realizes how extraordinarily steely it all is, how spendthrift even in its strength. When one looks at the plans, sees from the drafts and sketches (especially of some of the later plays) the meticulous process of re-designing that went on, one realizes that behind and within the outer cladding there is concealed a frame of invention of the highest tensile strength; one discovers not only the pillars of load-bearing realism but also a steel skeleton of poetic imagination. One sees how he shored up the fabric with further devices: buttresses of precise and meaningful stage-direction, scaffoldings of symbolism, motifs that appear decorative but which on examination are discovered also to be taking part of the strain, until the whole thing is braced and strutted into complete rigidity. Only thus was Ibsen able to use so imaginatively such unimaginative language, to compose dialogue that is so unnaturally natural, to make such a vivid impression with creations so uncompromisingly monochrome. It was none other than Maeterlinck—one of the least likely, it might seem, to find anything congenial in Ibsen—who detected this hidden thing; he listened to what he called "the inner dialogue," those exchanges conducted unspoken behind the spoken word, so eloquently inarticulate.

These dramas suppress their poetry as Brand suppressed his love, and from the same wilful strength. What is love (another of those things so conspicuously absent in Ibsen), says Brand with bitter scorn, but a cloak under which men conceal their lack of will; and what indeed, one might further ask, is hate in these plays but love turned sour—"If Mrs. Borkman had not loved her husband," Ibsen wrote in explanation of this figure of hate, "she would have forgiven him long ago." It seems that absence, and absence alone, makes the heart grow fonder, as one learns from Solveig's example, or from that of Martha in *Pillars of Society;* conversely, the closer the relationship, the more inevitable and bitter the estrangement. How loveless a thing is marriage in Ibsen's world: like Mrs. Alving's to be endured in shame; like Hedda Gabler's, a career in frustration; like the Master Builder's; even the children, Oswald, Hedvig, Little Eyolf, are blighted. There is infatuation in this world, possessiveness, appetite, there is amiability, reasonableness, devotion even; but one will search in vain for any love scene of genuine proportions, for any delicate exploration of personality by two people growing fond of each other.

What of those other deliberately contrived absences, those bare patches in the landscape that were not just left unpopulated but depopulated by design, empty spaces not just left out but carved out? There is in particular that fatal lack which disables the lives of so many of the characters, their essentially negative potential, by which as the result of some insufficiency, some incompetency, some impotence or inherent disqualification, some inauthenticity in the control or direction of their lives, they are so to speak debarred. Never has there been a gallery of lives so dedicated and yet so flawed, so disciplined and yet so unfulfilled, so determined and yet so insensible; lives so dedicated to All or Nothing, to homes for humans, to the good of society, to freedom under responsibility, to the compact majority, finding answers everywhere but in their own hearts; lives that under the pressure of dramatic event reveal (to use Eric Bentley's phrase) not unexpected depths but unexpected shallows.

They are, shall one say, shut away—but from what? From fortune? from happiness? from the truth? from self-fulfilment? Should one for the moment rather say: from the Light? Think of the imprisoned ones: like Hedda in the stuffy cell of her marriage to Tesman, a captive to bumbling amiability, dreaming of an admirer with vine leaves in his hair, and of the thrill of beautiful death; like Nora, placed under doll's house arrest, sneaking a few forbidden macaroons and squandering her life in deceiving her indulgent warder; like Oswald, kept in the dark about his wastrel father the whole of his young life and moaning for the sun; or like Borkman pacing up and down in his gallery like a caged animal. Think also of those who take refuge in a darkness of their own creating, who dwell in the shadow of a phrase or a lie or a secret dream: like Hjalmar Ekdal, comforted by the thought of the photographic invention he will never make; like Consul Bernick, sitting snug in the illusion that he is serving the community; like Alfred All-mers, sustained by the grandiose scheme of writing a big book on Human Responsibility. And here already one can see something that is strongly characteristic of Ibsen's dramatic utterances: the Light is something to play both hide *and* seek with; the Dark is either a prison or a refuge, something that shuts in or shuts out. On the other hand there are those words of Brand who tells of certain ideas (recurrent in Ibsen) that used to send him into fits of laughter: what if an owl were afraid of the dark, or a fish afraid of the water? How they would long for "air and the glad flames of day." And yet this (he says) is the lot of humankind, living between the fact of having to bear and the realization that it is unbearable; imprisoned. But then the Light, as well as being something to be yearned for, can also be something to be feared. In an early poem of Ibsen called "Fear of the Light," he confesses that his courage drains away as the sun rises, that the troubles of the day and the claims of life drip cold terror into his heart so that he hides himself under a flap of the scare-crow veil of the dark, embracing night as a protective shield.

Ibsen's benighted are thus of two main kinds: those who long for release, from oppressive respectability, from the commonplace, from frustration, who yearn for something wonderful to happen; and those others who take refuge from the insistent demands of life, who build up an insulation against the torments of decision and the agonies of conscience, whose approach to life is a retreat from it, a withdrawal into a stronghold of personal fantasy. And between them stand those who try to fill the fatal deficiency in their lives by taking from others, who illuminate their careers with borrowed light; those who apply themselves earnestly to the business of living but are inherently disqualified, who are like the African Magician in the Aladdin myth who covets the lamp that will assure his fortune but is debarred from seizing it unaided. Either, like Brand, they adopt some impersonal directive and live by code or statute because they cannot trust themselves to live by rule of thumb; or like Skule, whose sense of uncertainty is such that he doubts the very doubt that nags him and who takes over the "kingly thought" from his rival, they carry their deficiency about with them like a vacuum, desperately trying to fill it from without; but instead of filling it, they succeed only in encasing it in a shell of dedication, fastidiousness or borrowed authority; each stroke of the drama exhausts this vacuum a little more until at last the protective shell crumples under the pressure of external event.

What follows from this realization? The first thing is that these negative aspects of his work contribute materially to its achievement. It is certainly in part a technical *tour de force*, for it is in its own way as difficult to incorporate absent qualities in drama as it is to give examples of them in criticizing it. But it is also more. When Ibsen writes of the Light as something to yearn for and to flee from, of the Dark as something that oppresses and something that comforts, when he regards buildings as being both homes and cages, he is saying on the level of symbols what his dramas are often concerned to say dramatically: truth in *Pillars of Society* brings salvation, in *The Wild Duck* it brings destruction; a lie is synonymous with both an ideal and an illusion, something which for Hjalmar Ekdal makes life tolerable but which for Consul Bernick makes life intolerable. To ask for the essence of Ibsen, still more for the quintessence of Ibsenism, is to formulate a wholly misleading question; there is nothing to be got by boiling down, there is no extract of wisdom that would allow us to regard his drama as a linctus for the ills of mankind. If one must have an analogy, one might be a little nearer the truth by asking for the root of Ibsen; for just as the root of (say) 9 is not 3 but that more ambiguous entity mathematicians call ±3, so the root of Ibsen's view of life, however positively he may at times seem to express himself, conveys the impression of being similarly "plus or minus." The separate bits may not add up very satisfactorily, but they function.

The problem is then what sort of questions the modern Ibsenite should ask. One notices that in an age when literature gave itself to the business of debate, Ibsen himself waited for question time and cast his dramas in an interrogative mould. "I do but ask," he was fond of saying to those who sought enlightenment from him about the meaning of his works, "my call is not to answer." His dramas are those of one who understood the strategy of the contrived question and the shrewd supplementary, who knew how much more could be achieved by implication and insinuation and by the manner and timing of the asking than by the mere forcing of some answer. Perhaps his critics could learn from his example and acknowledge that there is room for an approach to Ibsen that questions the questions we ask of him rather than competes for answers. He offers a problem in delicate handling in which the matter of whether questions can be found to yield definite answers is subordinate to that of finding a genuinely Ibsenite question with the rightly provocative degree of obliquity. For example: Is there any Thing that might be discovered as standing to Ibsen as the Wild Duck stands to *The Wild Duck?*

Contemplating such Ibsenist Things, one wonders: How symbolic are they, and how are they symbolic, and are they all symbolic in the same way—the Wild Duck, the white horses in *Rosmersholm*, the sea in *The Lady from the Sea*, the "Indian Girl" in *Pillars of Society*, the infected baths, the orphanage, the high towers in *An Enemy of the People*, *Ghosts* and *The Master Builder?* What at one time it was sufficient to call a symbol (whether or not one felt inclined to add, like Arnold Bennett, "deplorable, even in its ingenuity") is now a "symbol,"

shielded by its quotation marks from any simple view that it might "stand for" anything in some straightforward sense; it is sometimes credited with explanatory or elucidatory power, sometimes with cohesive or magnetic force; at times it is seen as "a pressure point for all kinds of feeling," at times as a kind of appliance which gathers "all the scattered lights of the play and focuses them in one"; there is some suspicion that it is often attached to its play (and therefore "detachable") rather than inherently of it, that it is centrally placed rather than nuclear, perhaps even that it is intrinsic and extrinsic at one and the same time.

The Wild Duck is no doubt in one sense a centre of attraction; but it might be thought to have other and possibly more significant functions as a kind of formula or code word for finding the centre of gravity, the point about which all the separate elements exactly balance one another. Asked to imagine the shape of the play to which it belongs, one might see it as something equivocal, like a boomerang perhaps or a question mark, where the centre of gravity lies not within but without; but if one were to hang it up at any point, at Hedvig, say, or Hjalmar or Old Ekdal or the "life-lie" and allow things to find their natural equilibrium, this centre of gravity— although nothing more than a point in space—would come to rest immediately below the point of suspension; what one is not able to do is actually *balance* anything on this point of balance, this point which is detached and yet not strictly detachable, which is a function of the configuration of the piece rather than something of a piece with it. It would then be immaterial whether one hung the problem plays uppermost, or the visionary, or the poetic and non-theatrical; a private enthusiasm for, say, *A Doll's House* or *Ghosts* or *Peer Gynt* or even *Emperor and Galilean* (which would probably have been Ibsen's own choice) ought in theory all to point to the same spot.

Staring too fixedly, however, at the Wild

Duck has its dangers, and in straining the vision the analogy itself becomes strained. Looking round for a moment instead at the company it keeps, one becomes aware of another bird which has been strangely disregarded, one which along with Chekhov's Seagull seems to be—no matter what ornithology might say—a bird of a feather: Boccaccio's Falcon, that which appears in the ninth story of the fifth day of the *Decameron.* There is even some suggestion that the resemblance is not altogether accidental, the link between the two being Paul Heyse, German critic and author, whom Ibsen met in 1875 while living in Munich. Ibsen frequently attended the weekly meetings of the Crocodile Society, of which Heyse was a prominent member, and they saw much of each other without ever becoming close friends. A few years earlier, in 1871, Heyse had sketched his theory of the *Novelle,* his so-called *Falkentheorie,* derived from a study of Boccaccio's story; and it would be surprising if this did not on some occasion provide the society with something to discuss. Heyse had summed up his argument in the words: "Der Leser wird sich überall fragen, wo der Falke sei: also das Spezifische, das diese Geschichte von tausend anderen unterscheidet," i.e. look for the falcon, that which in some recognizable but not easily definable way focuses, particularizes, concretizes the work and gives it identity. A simple translation of Heyse's formula provides a paraphrase of the question implied above, a question in which Ibsen might have found quiet amusement, where the inner ramifications are everything and the answers largely incidental: Where is Ibsen's Wild Duck, that which distinguishes him from a thousand others?

The immediate past is not lacking in suggestions, many of which resemble each other only in their determination not to flatter. For James Joyce's Stephen Dedalus the differentia was cathartic: "You have," he said to the Ibsenite, "connected Ibsen and Eno's fruit salt for ever in my mind."

For Arne Garborg it was demonic, suggesting to him the figure of Trollman Whitebeard who spoke in riddles and acted so wise and turned the whole country into a madhouse by his magic. For Sir Walter Raleigh it was swinish: "I send you Zola and Ibsen," he wrote in a letter accompanying two very ugly cabinet photographs; ". . . they seem to me to embody modern earnestness, crankiness, gloom and stupidity in their speaking countenances. . . . I think we must frame them with the legend 'Modern Pigs' underneath." And Ibsen himself provided ammunition for his detractors by his reference to the Scorpion which preserved its health by injecting its poison into a piece of soft fruit: "Is there not a similarity," he wrote, "between this and writing poetry?" Many of the lyric poems, as well as the dramas themselves, make a contribution to the discussion, embodying in particular many of those more obvious and generally acknowledged qualities of their author: the profound and wholly pitiless psychological insight, the complex subtleties of organization, the stern judgement of individual responsibility, the scorn of inauthentic living and thinking. In the poems, the Strange Hunter on the *vidda* forces mortals to contemplate their lives "steel-set"; the Miner hammers his way into the secret chambers of the heart, ever deeper, seeking the answer to life's riddle, forgoing even the consolation of the light; and there is the suggestion of the Judge who holds doom sessions on the soul. Ibsen's astonishing technical skill invited identification with the Master Builder; and in view of Rubek's sardonic remarks in *When We Dead Awaken,* this might well be extended to include also a Master Sculptor:

There is something equivocal, something hidden within and behind these portraits—something private that the others cannot see. . . . I alone can see it. And I find it intensely amusing. Superficially there's the 'striking likeness,' as it is called, that people all stand gaping at in astonishment—but deeper down it is . . . just the dear old barnyard.

Nor should one neglect the Amazingly Clever Dog, the one that in any case fished up the Wild Duck from the depths—a Dog who (to put too fine a point on it, no doubt) was at first treated like a cur but lived to have the day the proverb promised him, who was fierce and bristling but who, if tossed a decoration by some crowned head, could be placated.

All these things are, however, too partial, too explicit, too "symbolic" in the sense that the Wild Duck is not; and when they are asked to accommodate some of the other less obvious but no less pervasive elements in these dramas, they fail. Where is the relevance to the incessant self-analysis of those characters who, as Hofmannsthal said, are forever thinking about thinking, feeling themselves feeling and conducting autopsychology; who think in slogans and long for the miraculous; who decorate their egocentric lives with secret dreams, subordinating all about them in private illusions of grandeur; whose lives are the deeds they have left undone, whose speech is the words they have left unspoken? Nor is it without relevance that these are explanations one makes in the study and not in the theatre; and many sensitive critics have insisted that it is only in the theatre that Ibsen should properly be judged. It is not good, they suggest, to go trudging down long avenues of reference every time Ibsen points his finger; there is, in the theatre, no time for digression, the pace has to be maintained. This was the view of James Joyce, whose early enthusiasm for Ibsen led him to teach himself Norwegian, the better to read the plays, who in March 1901 in his newly acquired foreign tongue wrote to Ibsen a very moving letter of homage and admiration, and who in an enthusiastic article on *When We Dead Awaken* in the *Fortnightly Review* of April 1900 claimed that "appreciation, hearkening, is the only true criticism":

If any plays demand a stage they are the plays of Ibsen. . . . They are so packed with thought. At some chance expression, the mind is tortured with some question, and in a flash long reaches of life are opened up in vista, yet the vision is momentary unless we stay to ponder it. It is just to prevent excessive pondering that Ibsen requires to be acted.

The real answer seems to be therefore that there is no answer; or rather that there is an infinity of answers too stark and stiff to fit anywhere but where they touch—which makes the modern Ibsenite's search for enlightenment a matter not of discovering some single secret truth but of rejecting a multiplicity of explanations which under scrutiny turn out to be inadmissible. Not even the precise ambiguity of the paradox nor the ambiguous precision of the "symbol" serve in the last resort to break down the complex unity of his art; he is irreducible.

Brian W. Downs

Love's Comedy and Ibsen's Humour

THESE pages have latterly been concerned for the most part with what may be called the positive content of the play. But it is not that which first and most insistently interests the reader or spectator of *Love's Comedy*. He is arrested and entertained before all else by the *negative* content, by the criticism and the satire of it, with which the brilliance of the dialogue and the crackle of the versification so perfectly accord. That it is satirical, Brandes remarked,[1] is the one thing in *Love's Comedy* on which all agree. In fact, the title may in itself be satirical. The "Farce of Love" would scarcely be even an ambiguous name for a play—and "Love's Comedy" is just possibly an analogue.

The nature, the aim and the implication of the satire have, however, been very variously interpreted. The disgruntled cleric Schack, who raked the sequence of Ibsen's masterpieces with steady volleys of moral objection, put his finger on the root of the difficulty when he complained[2] that the satirical lash is wielded by so dubious a person as Falk, "an incurable declaimer and phrase-monger." Falk *is* the mouthpiece of the satire; he may not be too harshly judged by Feilitzen when he calls him[3] "nothing but a harum-scarum rascal, even if an intelligent and idealistic rascal"; and, as has just been pointed out, Ibsen did

relegate him to a lower "stadium" than the people whom he criticised. That does not, however, necessarily invalidate his criticism. Thersites has some very pertinent things to say in *Troilus and Cressida*, things with which we may be sure that Shakespeare agreed; we need not on that account believe that Thersites everywhere speaks the last word, let alone identify Thersites with Shakespeare. It is much the same with Falk and Ibsen.

Against what, now, are Falk's satirical shafts directed? They are aimed at the customs of courtship and the conventional view of the married state obtaining in the better [4] middle-class society of Norway and at a more general attitude of mind underlying them; the shafts are sharp, they are well aimed and they strike home.[5]

It is unnecessary to expatiate at length on the apparition of Straamand, once wit and poet, now greasy priest and M.P., with his pregnant wife and eight little girls (four more at home), on the pedantic civil servant Styver, on the mummified virgin Frøken Skjære, on Fru Halm, who has so successfully managed her business of run-

[1] *Cit.* Schack, A., *Om Udviklingsgangen i Henrik Ibsens Digtning* (Kjøbenhavn, 1896), p. 30.
[2] Schack, *ut supra*, p. 21.
[3] *Ibsen och Äktenskapsfrågan* (Stockholm, 1882), p. 25.

[4] It is that: the stage direction at the head of Act II declares: "Well dressed ladies and gentlemen are drinking coffee on the verandah." Fru Halm's *pension* is on a grand scale; she has at least one man-servant and a *clientèle* comprising the flower of Norway's undergraduates.

[5] "*La Comédie de l'Amour* était la peinture indulgente et spirituellement philosophique de la situation singulière à laquelle une société maladroite condamne la passion" (Bigeon, M., *Les Révoltés Scandinaves*, 1894, p. 267).

From *A Study of Six Plays by Ibsen*, Cambridge University Press, 1950. Reprinted by permission. In a Prefatory Note, the author writes: "Except where otherwise stated, Ibsen's writings are quoted, by volume and page only, from the Standardutgave of his *Samlede Digter Verker* (7 volumes, Christiania, 1918) and, prefaced by the word 'Archer,' from the English *Collected Works of Henrik Ibsen* (edited by William Archer, 12 volumes, London, 1907–12; my thanks are due to Messrs Gyldendal and Messrs Heinemann for permission to do so."

ning a boarding-house as to approximate it to that of a procuress. Such are familiar and perennially amusing figures of light comedy, and Ibsen makes the most of them. What adds the barb of satire to the fun, what is intellectually interesting, is the circumstance that these people and the attitudes they take up are not necessarily to be looked on as comic or contemptible in themselves, in every light, as the duologues between Straamand and Falk and between Styver and Falk at the beginning of Act III are there to warn us; Ibsen does not insinuate—and not even the intelligent and idealistic Falk dares say—that married folk, even married parsons, should have no families, that there should be no formalities of betrothal and wedding, that it is wrong for persons who have plighted their troth to one another to remain faithful to it. No; these persons bare themselves to the satirist's shafts because their professions do not square with their behaviour, because they, all of them, commit a blunder just as egregious as and much more diverting than Falk's, but the *opposite* blunder. Whereas he, the aesthete, in courting Svanhild, is (part of the time at least) contemplating something that belongs to Kierkegaard's ethical stadium and for which he is congenitally unfit—entering upon the interminable obligations of marriage—*they* invest the solid and often homely realities of engagement and family life with the "aesthetic" flummery of romanticism. The urge to propagate and set up house, to have a comfortable home and a circle of friends, the wish to be quit of dependent, marriageable daughters, the instinct to stick to a mate once secured, dictated by physical and economic needs, they are always treated and mentioned by them as things in their nature both holy and beautiful, and everything which might indicate that they are not so and anyone who points out, for instance, that advancing years make even a lover fat and a mistress ugly, that the breeding of infants encourages squalor, that to be settled in life is detrimental to the wits, to the

charm and to the emotional sensibility of man and woman, is rounded upon for mere indecent blasphemy. On the one side there is the attitude embodied in Frøken Skjære with her flat declarations not only that love knows no gradations or shades, but also of the palpable absurdity that

> There is no *Want* where Love's the guiding star [6]

—as if a married couple had never starved to death in a garret. On the other side stands Falk's belief that, with its etiquette and regimentation, society has succeeded, so to speak, in codifying love away,[7] at any rate away from all the relations which it chooses to acknowledge. Says he:

> Love is with us a science and an art;
> It long since ceased to animate the heart.
> Love is with us a trade, a special line
> Of business, with its union, code and sign;
> It is a guild of married folks and plighted
> Past-masters with apprentices united.[8]

Falk is stung to his revolt by the incarnation of this antinomy, the spectacle of Straamand, his draggle-tail family, on whom Want can be no infrequent visitor, his unctuous complacency and complete intellectual and emotional nullity, when he contrasts it with the report of what Straamand once had been, namely, the Falk of his generation; the old Straamand is now stone dead—the corpse stinks, Falk gives plainly to understand;[9] yet all except himself unite

[6] 1, 286; Archer-Herford, 1, 309.
[7] Note that the representative of law and rule, Styver, congratulates himself (1, 277; Archer-Herford, 1, 291) on being *officially* engaged, something more, he knows, than being in love; his is the type of mind that automatically puts a Companion of Honour above a man of honour.
[8] Hos os er kærligheden snart en videnskab;
forlængst den hørte op at være lidenskab.
Hos os er kærligheden som et fag;
det har sit faste laug, sit eget flag;
den er en stand af kærester og ægtemænd. . . .
        (1, 329; Archer-Herford, 1, 398.)
This original, it will be noted, does not actually say anything about love being an *art*.
[9] 1, 347; Archer-Herford, 1, 430.

in Hosannas at its everlasting vitality, the
conspiracy being made no more excusable
for being animated by genuine self-deception.

Up to this point, the aspects of betrothal [10] and marriage on which the criticism of *Love's Comedy* fastens are fairly
harmless. But in one direction Ibsen goes
farther. Though Fru Halm's Anna seems a
nice enough young person, with the mak-
ings of a good wife and mother, Lind's engagement to her raises a storm in a teacup;
it is, however a real storm. Lind, the mild,
yet earnest student of divinity, urgently desires to administer spiritual consolations to
emigrants and, naturally, wants his wife to
accompany him into the Lord's vineyard.
But the life of a missionary and a missionary's wife is dangerous and unconventional; friends and aunts are at once mobi-
lized against the project, and, in the
warmth of recently crowned affection for
his bride, Lind consents, instead, to take
a post as an assistant-master in a girls'
academy.

The immediate clipping of the wings of
enterprise by matrimony is not merely un-
heroic, sad and, perhaps, slightly comic; it
can also amount to a crime. For Ibsen was
certain (and the certainty complicated his
own life by that self-debate on the real
value of art and the aesthete's life to which
reference was made above) that every man
or woman has a sense of vocation, a call
(Norwegian *kald*) to some occupation or
undertaking, and that under penalty of
spiritual death, he or she must follow the
call—at whatever sacrifice (Norwegian
offer). This dual point is driven home in
that *qui-pro-quo* (as the French stage tech-
nicality has it), where Falk and Straamand
hold forth about the two Norwegian words
in question:[11] the former understands by
kald and *offer* what Ibsen meant by them,

namely a personal sense of mission or function in life and a willingness to surrender
everything else to its demands, while the
portly cleric cannot think but that they
designate respectively the "call" which a
church-council might sound in the ear of a
candidate for ecclesiastical preferment and
the "offerings" at Easter, Pentecost and
Christmas with which the faithful substantiate their call. In his use of the terms,
Straamand incurs the guilt that Ibsen was
so plentifully castigating in the play, giving
vague, high-sounding names to what, however necessary, is purely utilitarian.

Owing to the cleverness of its verse and
the grotesquerie of some of the personages
—the coincidence that the entire Straamand progeny should be female, for instance, or Styver's inability to express himself except in the style of the chancery—the
satirical tone rings clearer perhaps through
Love's Comedy than through any other of
Ibsen's plays—though there is the delicious,
artificial figure of the *norsk-norsk* champion Paulsen in the early *St. John's Eve* to
bear in mind, who has "gone all folkly"· and
shows it not only by wearing a dirk on
his thigh, but by his heroic gesture of defiance in spelling nouns without capital
letters.

Satire implying humour or wit (or
both), one should turn for examples of it
rather to an author's comedies than to
dramas or tragedies. After his nonage,
Ibsen wrote at any rate two plays allowed
by general consent to rank as comedies:
they are *The League of Youth* (*De Unges
Forbund*, 1869) and *An Enemy of the
People* (*En Folkefiende*, 1882). The two
disclose certain striking resemblances, the
plainest being their bold trenching on the
domain of politics, the contemporary politics of Norway. A further point at which
The League of Youth and *An Enemy of the
People* approximate and which, moreover,
Love's Comedy has in common with them is
the volubility of the chief character. But
here the parallel must not be drawn too far.

---

[10] The humours of betrothal had been given full
scope in Heiberg's comedy, *De Uadskillige*, and
the antics of engaged couples had been repellent
enough to break a match in Kierkegaard's *For-
førerens Dagbog*.

[11] 1, 313; Archer-Herford, 1, 366.

It is commonly assumed, indeed, that Dr. Thomas Stockmann, Public Enemy Number One,[12] because he has his windows broken and his livelihood taken from him, should be looked on as a completely admirable martyr in the causes of individualism and professional integrity. That is going too far. He is a figure of fun; and traits in his character were copied by Ibsen from his great contemporary Bjørnstjerne Bjørnson, of whom he by no means wholly approved, and from the novelist Jonas Lie,[13] a worthy man indeed, but a debater as confused as he was excited and sincere. Nevertheless, Ibsen's satire in *An Enemy of the People* is not mainly centred on Dr. Stockmann, as that of *The League of Youth* is on Stensgaard, and, according to one possible view, that of *Love's Comedy* on its protagonist Falk.

Even if Dr. Stockmann, unlike Stensgaard and perhaps Falk, is not the chief butt of the play in which he appears, the general considerations suggested by all three figures stress a definite and vital resemblance. In *Love's Comedy*, in *The League of Youth* and in *An Enemy of the People*, whoever may be the main target of criticism, Ibsen directs the point of his attack at the discrepancy between word and deed, at slogans, catch-phrases, pet notions and loud-mouthed professions which falsify the reality supposedly represented by them. About this aspect of *Love's Comedy* enough should have been said. The League of Youth is ostensibly to sweep away the stuffiness and jobbery of "the old gang," but it is actually called into existence to provide an adventurer with a seat in parliament and a rich wife; in *An Enemy of the People* the "compact Liberal majority" repress disinterested investigation and free speech, while actively conniving at the ill-health of

that community whose good is ever on their lips, in so transparently hypocritical a manner as to prove comic as well as sinister.[14]

Thus it comes that Ibsen's satire is so largely directed against those who live by their powers of expression [15]—politicians like Peter Stockmann and the gross of *The League of Youth*, lawyers like Stensgaard, newspaper-men like Billing and Hovstad of *An Enemy of the People* and Mortensgaard of *Rosmersholm*, clergymen like Pastor Manders of *Ghosts* and Molvik of *The Wild Duck*, poets like Falk,[16] schoolmasters like Rørlund of *The Pillars of Society* and Arnholm of *The Lady from the Sea*, even a chancery-stylist like Styver. The animus moreover which he exhibited against the Liberal party, with whose principles, after all, he was usually in much greater accord than with those of the Conservatives whom Peter Stockmann represents, was due to his believing the Liberals to be *par excellence* the party of gas-bags. As soon as Johan Sverdrup's party stopped carping in opposition and, grasping the reins of government in Norway,[17] showed that they could exercise authority, he toned down his fleers at them.[18]

Humour is about the last attribute with which general fame would endow our author.[19] But the common view of Ibsen as

[14] *Peer Gynt* unrolls too vast a canvas to describe merely in a footnote to another work, but it may here be observed that its hero is another great *Maulheld* or "jaw-hero" (as the countrymen of Hitler called such), and that the way, so to put it, in which his "jaw" messes up his life and character furnishes an essential theme.

[15] Ibsen did so himself: irony at his own expense is by no means to be ruled out.

[16] No doubt a little salutary self-chastisement was therewith intended.

[17] In 1884.

[18] Of course Mortensgaard's "limited liability" radicalism in *Rosmersholm* (1886), for which Sverdrup's government afforded parallels, does not escape scatheless; the advocate of bold measures is as timid as the "gentlemen's party" is caddish.

[19] Saintsbury, G., *The Later Nineteenth Century* (Edinburgh, 1907), p. 321, speaks of his constant "demand that such a thing as humour shall be banished from his world."

[12] That would be the equivalent of "Folkefiende" in the English jargon of to-day, rather than "Enemy of the People."

[13] The same who was proprietor and editor of *Illustreret Nyhedsbald*, when it printed *Love's Comedy*, and who paid Kr. 400 for the copyright.

a "gloomy sort of ghoul, bent on groping for horrors by night, and blinking like a stupid old owl when the warm sunlight of the best of life dances into his wrinkled eyes," which *The Gentlewoman* advanced,[20] is altogether beside the mark. *Love's Comedy* fits in uncommonly ill with such a definition. By itself, that piece should dispel any notion that if Ibsen ever produced comic effects it was by inadvertence or incompetence. Many such effects in that play belong of course to the stock-in-trade of light comedy: the cleric whose paunch and large family (possibly, a red nose too) proclaim his carnal proclivities;[21] the young things' aunts, whose unanimity of conventional utterance possesses the mechanical quality of a chorus; the civil servant who cannot speak except in terms of his mystery (and who goes about in the futile endeavour to renew the promissory note so ubiquitous in mid-nineteenth-century literature [22]) ; the *qui-pro-quo* or the protracted misunderstanding through which at one time Falk thinks Lind has snapped away his Svanhild and at another Lind believes Guldstad to be after his Anna, as well as the verbal confusions concerning *offer* and *kald* already alluded to. But even these hack devices (except perhaps the business of Styver's promissory note) are treated freshly, as things really seen by the author in a live setting, and are given a crispness and variety by the wit of the dialogue and an ingenuity in rhyming which are altogether Ibsen's own. A French critic has even accorded the supreme praise of attributing "Latin grace" to them.[23]

In private life, Ibsen possessed a genuine sense of humour. Holberg, the "Molière of the North," was his favourite author. One who met him about 1880 reports [24] that he liked little jokes, even coarse jokes, and regretted that the latter were inadmissible in literature. He himself certainly neither made capital of his sense of humour nor gave rein to it. Report has it [25] that as a child he was sometimes in the literal sense, convulsed with laughter, his body heaving and shaking while no sound burst from his lips—and a humour, of course, of which the manifestations are rigorously suppressed may come near to being no humour at all. Again, Ibsen's humour undoubtedly had in general a saturnine quality which, to the tender-hearted, just as effectively nullifies it; he used, it is said, to divert himself with the imagined predicament of a fish that had incurred hydrophobia, and the joke is made no more palatable to some when he likened man, with his passion for ideals, to such a fish. His humour may be thought of as lightning against an angry sky, rather than the sunny, smiling champaign of a Sterne.

Exactly how much humour may be imputed to Ibsen, since it is as little blatant as may be, will depend largely on the interpretation of the plays as well as on the observer's own fondness for the sardonic and ironical. *The Lady from the Sea* may be taken as an illustration of this. To some it is as tragic as *Hedda Gabler*. But according to another explanation, it is a genuine comedy: a lady is radically cured of some half-crazy notions, to which debased romantic ideas have attached a certain reverence, and through that cure a tippling husband and two neglected daughters are saved from going utterly to the bad; the cure is effected partly by moral prescrip-

---

[20] *Auct.* Shaw, G. B., *Quintessence of Ibsenism* (3rd ed., London, 1922), p. 89.

[21] On the one hand it may be observed that the anomaly would not be so striking in Norway as in some countries, as the Lutheran is the least "other-worldly" type of Christianity; on the other hand Herford (*Fortnightly Review,* February 1900, p. 193) is probably right in asserting that this was the first time a clergyman had been profaned by the Norwegian boards and the effect of his appearance on them would be extremely startling.

[22] Cf. *Plain or Ringlets?*, *Père Goriot, Framley Parsonage,* etc.

[23] Bigeon, M., *Les Révoltés Scandinaves* (1894), p. 267.

[24] Grønwald, M., *Fra Ulrikken til Alperne* (1925), p. 145.

[25] *Auct.* Koht, H., *Henrik Ibsen,* 1 (Oslo, 1928), p. 24.

tion (by bestowing on an irresponsible, but not otherwise worthless, person responsibility with freedom to act), partly, too, by a disillusionment, which has a definitely comic aspect: a Stranger, who had appeared to a half-grown girl like some monstrous merman, with nameless crimes, temptations and fascination about his personality, magnified in her imagination a thousand times by the intervening years of undistracted day-dreaming, makes his appearance at last as a participant in a Cook's Tour to the Midnight Sun, sporting red bushy whiskers, a tam-o'-shanter on his pate and a hold-all attached to his person. The more obviously neglected of the two daughters, moreover, is endowed with a sardonic humour akin to her creator's: a pure aesthete, she lives, like any disciple of Walter Pater, in order to get as many pulsations as possible into her given time and to this end she finds a peculiar fascination in leading on the young sculptor Lyngstrand; she tempts him to expatiate on his callow ambitions, knowing them to be chimerical, since phthisis will have laid him in the grave long before he has any chance of realising them. Even if, in her sister's words, she is dismissed as "really a horrid child," that does not dispose of Lyngstrand's fatuity, though individual taste will vary in the lengths to which it will go with his sardonic observer in deriving entertainment from it.[26]

It remains true, of course, that Ibsen's serious plays have no deliberately planned "comic relief" and that, whatever their comic implications, the situations themselves are rarely comic and, when comic, only mildly so. The momentary misunderstanding of Lona Hessel (in *Pillars of Society*), that the respectable sewing party

into which, behind drawn blinds, she has intruded, is a bevy of repentant Magdalenes, may be thought typical, or the joy of poor old Foldal (*John Gabriel Borkman*) at his daughter's luck, when he has been all but run down by the sleigh in which she is driving as one of an extremely dubious *partie à trois*. The three courtships of Lawyer Stensgaard with all the shifts and misunderstandings to which their simultaneity gives rise show that Ibsen was capable of planning this sort of thing on a large scale—and *The League of Youth*, which is built up exclusively on broadish satire and complicated dramatic intrigue; has for nearly eighty years been a "box-office draw" in the North, much as *The Private Secretary* in England.

Of comic characters, however, Ibsen commands a greater plenitude than of comic situations, though their number rather notably declines at the end of his career, after *The Lady from the Sea*, so that *The Master Builder* [27] and *When We Dead Awaken* contain none; *John Gabriel Borkman* has only the ghost of a pathetic smile evoked by poor Vilhelm Foldal, and *Little Eyolf* the grotesque and sinister Rat Wife, who can scarcely have been intended to raise even the ghost of a smile. Before these —even as late as *Hedda Gabler*, with the footling scholar Tesman—Ibsen provides sketches for quite a fair-sized gallery of comic character-portrayals. *The Wild Duck* is perhaps richest in them,[28] with the Dickensian Lieutenant Ekdal,[29] mighty

[26] Again, some, seduced by the beauty of Grieg's music, have seen in *Peer Gynt* a kind of second *Faust*, set in hyperborean mists and uncouthness, with a fevered Saharan nightmare taking the place of the Hellenic interlude; but perhaps it is they, with Anitra and Begriffenfeldt and The Lean One before them, who lack a sense of humour and not the author.

[27] Of course there is something grimly comic, not lost on young Brovik and his friends, about the Master Builder himself, who cannot climb his own towers (and breaks his neck trying to do so).
[28] "I remember," says Bernard Shaw (*Quintessence of Ibsenism*, 3rd ed., London, 1922), "a performance of *The Wild Duck*, at which the late Clement Scott pointed out triumphantly that the play was so absurd that even the champions of Ibsen could not help laughing at it. It had not occurred to him that Ibsen could laugh like other men."
[29] Relling, who, I think, must be trusted throughout, declares "the old lieutenant has been an ass all his days," and the great actor Olaf Paulsen,

hunter of tame rabbits before the Lord, with the "demoniac" drunkard of a parson, Molvik, and with the incomparable Hjalmar himself, who, while his heart is supposed to be broken, his brain in a whirl and his honour outraged, plaintively gropes about the lunch-table for more butter.[30] Besides these, to name but a few, there is the grandiloquent philosopher of the casual ward, Ulrick Brendel (*Romersholm*); there are the malicious grotesques, Daniel Hejre of *The League of Youth* and Morten Kiil of *An Enemy of the People*, parts well recognised in the countries where Ibsen has a place in the theatres' permanent repertory as highly rewarding to the actor; there is Peer Gynt, the Playboy of the Northern World; there is Dr. Thomas Stockmann; there is the quite preposterous standard-bearer of the ideal, Hilmar Tønnesen (*Pillars of Society*), whose banner seems to bear the strange device "Fennimore Cooper." The proximity of many of these personages to tragedy adds piquancy to their absurdities. The interaction between a

---

who so largely secured the success of the piece at Copenhagen, always acted him very broadly, after the style of the chuckle-headed countrymen of Fritz Reuter's novels.

[30] It is to be observed how in all these cases the comic effect is repeatedly obtained by the contrast between profession and conduct.

potentially comic character [31] and an incongruous situation is nowhere better exhibited than in the scene in *Ghosts* where the rascally hypocrite Engstrand, by his glib obsequiousness, not merely disarms the Reverend Mr. Manders's just indignation against him, but even induces him to serve as patron to the house of ill-fame which he proposes to set up with the extremely double-edged name of "Chamberlain Alving's Home for Seamen."

In the above catalogue only one female figured—to be rejected at once—namely the Rat Wife of *Little Eyolf*. Ibsen did not go in much for funny women or for comic situations in which women play an important part, unless we do young Hilde Wangel the honour of ranking her as a woman. No doubt, as with her prototype Aasta Hanstein,[32] there is good fun to be extracted from the appearance and mannerisms of Lona Hessel in *The Pillars of Society*, but the only feminine character a theatrical manager would be moved to "cast" directly as a comic one is Madam Rundholmen of *The League of Youth*, a much attenuated Mistress Quickly.

[31] I can still recall the "high light" of Eleonora Duse's acting of *Spettri*, on her last visit to London, when she let Helene Alving break into silvery laughter at the "grande bambino, Pastore Manders."

[32] Painter and militant upholder of women's rights (and wrongs) in the Norway of the 1870's.

Raymond Williams

Ibsen's Non-Theatrical Plays

"FAME," said Rilke, "is the sum of misunderstanding which gathers about a new name." The English, indeed the European, fame of Ibsen is perhaps a case in point. Almost everywhere one is told that Ibsen wrote plays about the social problems of his day, and that the typical Ibsen manner is that of the conversational play, in which every character is provided with a family, and every room with heavy furniture, a certain stuffiness in the air, and a secret mouldering in the corner cupboard. These ideas about Ibsen spring from a mistake of emphasis which, in England, began with the London performances of *A Doll's House* in 1889, and of *Ghosts* and *Hedda Gabler* in 1891. These plays—*Ghosts* in particular—were hysterically abused by a "compact majority" of the reviewers and right-thinking men of the day. Mr Clement Scott compared *Ghosts* to, among other things, "an open drain" and "a dirty act done publicly"; Ibsen was "a raven . . . with an insatiable appetite for decayed flesh." Scott's outbursts are distinguished from others only by the lack of restraint encouraged by a fluent pen and a waiting press.

It is best, of course, in such cases, if no attempt is made at defence. Since the attacks are irrelevant, defence will only give away the artist's case. For Ibsen, there were too many defenders. Ibsenism and Ibsenites sprang up everywhere. Mr Shaw wrote *The Quintessence of Ibsenism*, having, it seems, decided quite firmly in advance what the plays ought to mean. What Shaw expounded in his book was hardly what Ibsen had written in his plays. But the Ibsenite emphasis on subject, as something which could be considered apart from the words of the play, was characteristic; and it was very welcome to the many people who wanted, not a dramatist, but a moral leader. The effect of this emphasis was to centre attention on elements in Ibsen which were in fact incidental: on the emancipation of women and the freedom of youth; on the "whited sepulchres" of Christian fathers and gentlemen; on the slam of Nora Helmer's front door which "brought down behind it in dust the whole Victorian family gallery." These things made the scandal, and, in the way of scandals, they made the success; they made Ibsen. And it became impossible for anyone to think about Ibsen at all except in terms of that initial public impression. To a larger extent than we may realise, this is still the case. The result is that many of his plays are still misunderstood, both in reading and on the stage.

The part of Ibsen's career which is almost universally neglected, but which I think it is essential to study, is the six years from 1851 to 1857, during which he worked as a dramatist, producer and stage manager in the small struggling theatre at Bergen, and the seven following years in which he was attached to theatres in Christiania. While Ibsen was at Bergen, 145 plays were produced, and 75 of them were French. The typical production was the play of romantic intrigue, of which Scribe was the leading exponent. The success of such a play depended on a complicated plot, moving at high speed around certain stock scenes: the confidential docu-

First published in *The Listener*, 22 December 1949, and subsequently adapted and incorporated into *Drama from Ibsen to Eliot*, Chatto and Windus, London, 1952. Reprinted by permission.

ment dropped in public, for example; or the abducted baby identified by a secret birthmark; or the poisoned goblet passing from hand to hand and being drunk in the end by anyone but the intended victim. Action had become mere spectacle, without any important dramatic function. One of Ibsen's earliest critical remarks refers scornfully to the "dramatic sweetmeats of Scribe and company." None the less, his own plays of this period follow the prescribed spectacular pattern. *Lady Inger of Ostraat*, for example, is a typical intrigue play. The fact is that although he recognized the limitations of the intrigue play as drama, he knew from the daily experience of production under his own hands how skilfully contrived was such a play for theatrical success.

Ibsen, however, could not be content to go on writing "for stock." As his art matured, he found it more and more impossible to express anything of importance under this tyranny of theatrical form. In 1864, when he was thirty-six, he abandoned the attempt at compromise. The theatre was stifling his dramatic intentions. He would go on writing drama, but he would not write it for the theatre. *Brand* and *Peer Gynt* were the immediate product of this decision. Each was composed in conscious disregard of the theatre in which Ibsen was skilled. And this disregard was not for the sake of "realism." *Brand* and *Peer Gynt* were both written in verse; in both, the scenic limits of the stage were ignored. Further, both *Brand* and *Peer Gynt* reveal in a remarkable way the central themes of Ibsen's dramatic writing. In Brand's unswerving devotion to his ministry, in Peer's aimless drift towards what he calls "Selfhood," the keyword, as in the earlier play *The Pretenders*, is *vocation, calling*. That Brand's calling is religious is not, as Ibsen explained, the important point: "the demand," he added, "might be made anywhere." The very last thing, in fact, that the play could be is the "satire on religious mania" which Mr Shaw tried to make of it.

Brand's wholehearted response to his call is justified in contrast with the "partial men" who have "no virtue whole." Absolute response to the call is the only self-fulfilment that matters. But the ability to respond is limited by the actual human situation. Brand is increasingly weighed down by inherited spiritual debts: the debt through the pagan Gerd from his mother; the current obligations of responsibility to his wife and child; and, above all, the general human debt—the birth sin. Brand's words, in failure, are "Blood of children must be spilt, To atone for parents' guilt."

This, in Ibsen, is the recurrent human failure. It is the failure, not only of Brand, but of Oswald in *Ghosts*, of Little Eyolf, of Hedvig in *The Wild Duck*, and even of Hedda Gabler. The only reassurance comes from the voice which calls through the avalanche: "He is the God of Love." Peer Gynt, similarly, inherits from his wastrel father and his defeated mother the debt which governs his life—the patterns of fantasy. When the Button-Moulder comes to collect Peer, to return him as scrap to the casting-ladle, Peer asks, "What is it to be oneself?" "It is to stand forth everywhere," he is answered, "with the Master's intention clearly displayed. Now you," the Button-Moulder adds, "you were designed for a shining button, on the coat of the world, but your loop gave way." Peer, in fact, has followed the Boyg's advice and, in the habit of his mother's tales to him as a child, "gone round about." Brand had refused to "go round about," and he had been destroyed. Peer's fate is different. In failing to answer his call he has failed also to become himself. He is a wasted life, scrap to be melted down for a new moulding. At the last moment Peer is able, nevertheless, to be saved, through Solveig, for "the father forgives at the mother's prayer."

It seems to me that it was the expression of these recurrent themes, rather than any social purpose or any intentions in realism, which led Ibsen to reject the romantic theatre and to undertake his many experiments. An important artist is not likely to look for a new technique for its own sake; the innovation is determined by the experience. Ibsen's work, from this time on, is remarkable for the uniformity of its experience. The necessity of responding to vocation; the conviction that such response is limited by the "heritage of debt"; the returning fear that direct and spontaneous living—"joy in the beautiful life of earth," as Peer Gynt had put it—has been sacrificed to responsibility and to a conscious purpose in life: these themes preoccupy his maturity. Julian, in *Emperor and Galilean,* is "sacrificed to his life's design," but is absolved by the Christian Makrina. Even *Ghosts,* which some people refer to as a play about a social problem, is a striking dramatic realisation of the destruction of a calling by an inherited human debt. Brand has said of men:

> Born to be tenants of the deep,
> Born to be exiles from the sun,
> Crying to heaven, in vain we pray,
> For air and the glad flames of day.

The Emperor Julian had died crying, "O Sun, O Helios, why hast thou forsaken me?" Oswald dies crying in vain for "the sun, the sun." The issues are constant, but there is some variation in Ibsen's attitude towards them. At times, as in *The Lady from the Sea* (Ellida is another "tenant of the deep"), the inherited debt can, like an evil spirit, be exorcised; can even, in the scientific manner, be cured. More often, and finally, the debt must be redeemed with a life.

But these preoccupations were not, for Ibsen, problems in the sense of the "problem play." "Everything which I have written I have lived through," he said, "I never wrote because I had, as they say, found a good subject." Ibsen, that is to say, was not interested in Heredity, but in the experience of inheritance. He was not interested in Idealism but in the experience of calling. There are, it is true, parts of *Brand* where the experience seems dissociated. The Brand of the earlier acts has the crude lines

of a theoretical creature. He has, it would seem, no roots; not because the experience which contains him is inorganic or insubstantial, but because it is now, as communicated, rootless; it has been dug up and exhibited at the level of conscious debate. Brand's sermon in Act Five on weakness and freedom is as much a failure of discipline as the now faded topical satire of the fourth act of *Peer Gynt.* But the last act of *Brand,* and in a greater degree the last act of *Peer Gynt,* have the substantial quality of poetic drama.

In *Brand* the dramatic imagery of dove and falcon is magnificently controlled. The dove and the falcon have been closely interwoven throughout the poem. The dove which will descend has been the ultimate Love; when "will" has conquered, the dove brings life. The falcon, on the other hand, has been identified with sin. Brand recalls "a childish scene that still lives in the mind . . . like a festering wound," the scene of his mother robbing the bed of his dead father, swooping "down like a falcon on her prey." The falcon, also, has been shown as "the spirit of compromise," which Brand also calls the devil. In the last scene Gerd, the pagan girl, shoots at the falcon on the peak which she calls the ice-church. "I have hit him," she shouts:

> Plumes in thousands from his breast,
> Flutter down the mountainside.
> See how large he looms, how white. . . .
> He is white, see, as a dove.

It is the avalanche, which the shot has begun. "The mountains crumble." For Brand it is the meeting point of sin and redemption, which the falcon and the dove have embodied, and which Gerd has identified. The fifth act of *Peer Gynt* rests on a complex pattern of images of the same kind, some of which, like the Button-Moulder, are dramatically conceived as characters. The folk-material and the legends which went to the making of *Peer Gynt* have given it a richer and more dramatically compelling substance than the rather angular material which Ibsen called "the syllogism of

Brand." The fifth act of *Peer Gynt* is virtually complete in itself, and seems to me to be the highest point of Ibsen's achievement in drama.

Brand and *Peer Gynt*—Ibsen's non-theatrical plays—are the works on which, in my view, his status as a dramatist depends. Yet when he had written them, he set himself to a different order of drama. "My new play," he wrote of *The League of Youth,* "will be in prose, and in every way adapted for the stage." He wishes, he says, "to create the illusion of reality," and he did not notice the unconscious irony of the phrase. He even attacked the use of verse on the stage, and predicted that the drama of the near future would have little use for it. But it is a mistake to suppose that this was his final attitude. In 1884 he wrote: "I certainly remember that I once expressed myself disrespectfully with regard to verse, but that was a result of my own momentary attitude. I have long since ceased to set up principles of general application, because I no longer believe that such principles can be set up." Meanwhile, however, he refined his skill "to create the illusion of reality." *The Wild Duck, Rosmersholm, Hedda Gabler* are impressively worked. But the words of the plays increasingly imply, rather than state, their dramatic sense. The form is still that of the drama, but the manner is that of the novel. The plays depend increasingly on acting which is only loosely controlled by the words, and on devices of visual atmosphere—what are called Ibsen's symbols.

One could hardly fail to admire the workmanship of a play like *Rosmersholm,* but the prose plays seem to me less interesting *as drama* than those works which he wrote when he was not bothering about making a play to fit the realistic theatre of the time. These naturalist plays, I would say, are really just a fictional refinement—I grant that the refinement is considerable—of the old romantic drama in which Ibsen had been schooled. The devices of the romantic drama are frequently used: *A Doll's House* turns on a fatal document—Krogstad's note; *The Wild Duck* turns on an authentic fatal secret. Even the discussion scene, which Mr Shaw takes as a sure sign of the New Drama, is simply the *scène à faire* of the French romantic theatre. The dialogue of *Hedda Gabler,* on the other hand, is so much that of a novel that, without commentary, it is hardly ever realised that the play is essentially a kind of farce, and its ending deliberate bathos.

But once again Ibsen turned from the theatre. In 1891, when he was sixty-three, he began the series of last plays, culminating in *John Gabriel Borkman* and *When We Dead Awaken.* The atmosphere is again that of *Brand* and *Peer Gynt* and the limits of the realistic stage are ignored. Rubek, the artist in *When We Dead Awaken,* knows that he has missed "the beautiful life of earth." He has come "to a tight place where you stick fast, you cannot move forward or backward." Like Brand, he dies under the avalanche, and a voice cries "Peace be with you." It is sometimes objected that the characters of *When We Dead Awaken* are bloodless. But that is their spiritual condition, not a technical failure by the dramatist. Ibsen indeed, in this play, uses a dramatic method which Strindberg and the German expressionists were to follow with considerable success: where the character is stripped of all that is judged irrelevant, and is seen, not as a person, but as an element in a dramatic pattern.

When we come, finally, to value Ibsen, we must, I think, set him, not among the "social dramatists" who have been taken as his disciples, but primarily among the writers of poetic drama. Where he will stand among writers of this order is uncertain, although it can hardly be in the first rank. But this final act of valuation is a very difficult one; because, in order to make it, we are really called upon to value something of which we are still a part; something which, more than any other man, Ibsen created: the consciousness of modern European drama.

Francis Fergusson

Ghosts

GHOSTS is not Ibsen's best play, but it serves my purpose, which is to study the foundations of modern realism, just because of its imperfections. Its power, and the poetry of some of its effects, are evident; yet a contemporary audience may be bored with its old-fashioned iconoclasm and offended by the clatter of its too-obviously well-made plot. On the surface it is a *drame à thèse,* of the kind Brieux was to develop to its logical conclusion twenty years later: it proves the hollowness of the conventional bourgeois marriage. At the same time it is a thriller with all the tricks of the Boulevard entertainment: Ibsen was a student of Scribe in his middle period. But underneath this superficial form of thesis-thriller—the play which Ibsen started to write, the angry diatribe as he first conceived it—there is another form, the shape of the underlying action, which Ibsen gradually made out in the course of his two-years' labor upon the play, in obedience to his scruple of truthfulness, his profound attention to the reality of his fictive characters' lives. The form of the play is understood according to two conceptions of plot, which Ibsen himself did not at this point clearly distinguish: the rationalized concatenation of events with a univocal moral, and the plot as the "soul" or first actualization of the directly perceived action.

Halvdan Koht, in his excellent study *Henrik Ibsen,* has explained the circumstances under which *Ghosts* was written. It was first planned as an attack upon marriage, in answer to the critics of *A Doll's House.* The story of the play is perfectly coherent as the demonstration and illustration of this thesis. When the play opens, Captain Alving has just died, his son Oswald is back from Paris where he had been studying painting, and his wife is straightening out the estate. The Captain had been accepted locally as a pillar of society but was in secret a drunkard and debauchee. He had seduced his wife's maid, and had a child by her; and this child, Regina, is now in her turn Mrs. Alving's maid. Mrs. Alving had concealed all this for something like twenty years. She was following the advice of the conventional Pastor Manders and endeavoring to save Oswald from the horrors of the household: it was for this reason she had sent him away to school. But now, with her husband's death, she proposes to get rid of the Alving heritage in all its forms, in order to free herself and Oswald for the innocent, unconventional "joy of life." She wants to endow an orphanage with the Captain's money, both to quiet any rumors there may be of his sinful life and to get rid of the remains of his power over her. She encounters this power, however, in many forms, through the Pastor's timidity and through the attempt by Engstrand (a local carpenter who was bribed to pretend to be Regina's father) to blackmail her. Oswald wants to marry Regina and has to be told the whole story. At last he reveals that he has inherited syphilis from his father—the dead hand of the past in its most sensationally ugly form—and when his brain softens at the end, Mrs. Alving's whole plan collapses in unrelieved horror. It is "proved" that she should have left

From *The Idea of a Theater*, Princeton University Press, 1949; reprinted in Doubleday Anchor Books, New York. Used by permission.

home twenty years before, like Nora in *A Doll's House;* and that conventional marriage is therefore an evil tyranny.

In accordance with the principles of the thesis play, *Ghosts* is plotted as a series of debates on conventional morality, between Mrs. Alving and the Pastor, the Pastor and Oswald, and Oswald and his mother. It may also be read as a perfect well-made thriller. The story is presented with immediate clarity, with mounting and controlled suspense; each act ends with an exciting curtain which reaffirms the issues and promises important new developments. In this play, as in so many others, one may observe that the conception of dramatic form underlying the thesis play and the machine-made Boulevard entertainment is the same: the logically concatenated series of events (intriguing thesis or logical intrigue) which the characters and their relationships merely illustrate. And it was this view of *Ghosts* which made it an immediate scandal and success.

But Ibsen himself protested that he was not a reformer but a poet. He was often led to write by anger and he compared the process of composition to his pet scorpion's emptying of poison; Ibsen kept a piece of soft fruit in his cage for the scorpion to sting when the spirit moved him. But Ibsen's own spirit was not satisfied by the mere discharge of venom; and one may see, in *Ghosts,* behind the surfaces of the savage story, a partially realized tragic form of really poetic scope, the result of Ibsen's more serious and disinterested brooding upon the human condition in general, where it underlies the myopic rebellions and empty clichés of the time.

In order to see the tragedy behind the thesis, it is necessary to return to the distinction between plot and action, and to the distinction between the plot as the rationalized series of events, and the plot as "the soul of the tragedy." The action of the play is "to control the Alving heritage for my own life." Most of the characters want some material or social advantage from it

—Engstrand money, for instance, and the Pastor the security of conventional respectability. But Mrs. Alving is seeking a true and free human life itself—for her son, and through him, for herself. Mrs. Alving sometimes puts this quest in terms of the iconoclasms of the time, but her spiritual life, as Ibsen gradually discovered it, is at a deeper level; she tests everything—Oswald, the Pastor, Regina, her own moves—in the light of her extremely strict if unsophisticated moral sensibility: by direct perception and not by ideas at all. She is tragically seeking; she suffers a series of pathoses and new insights in the course of the play; and this rhythm of will, feeling, and insight underneath the machinery of the plot is the form of the life of the play, the soul of the tragedy.

The similarity between *Ghosts* and Greek tragedy, with its single fated action moving to an unmistakable catastrophe, has been felt by many critics of Ibsen. Mrs. Alving, like Oedipus, is engaged in a quest for her true human condition; and Ibsen, like Sophocles, shows on-stage only the end of this quest, when the past is being brought up again in the light of the present action and its fated outcome. From this point of view Ibsen is a plot-maker in the first sense: by means of his selection and arrangement of incidents he defines an action underlying many particular events and realized in various modes of intelligible purpose, of suffering, and of new insight. What Mrs. Alving sees changes in the course of the play, just as what Oedipus sees changes as one veil after another is removed from the past and the present. The underlying form of *Ghosts* is that of the tragic rhythm as one finds it in *Oedipus Rex.*

But this judgment needs to be qualified in several respects: because of the theater for which Ibsen wrote, the tragic form which Sophocles could develop to the full, and with every theatrical resource, is hidden beneath the clichés of plot and the surfaces "evident to the most commonplace mind." At the end of the play the tragic rhythm of Mrs. Alving's quest is not so much completed as brutally truncated, in obedience to the requirements of the thesis and the thriller. Oswald's collapse, before our eyes, with his mother's screaming, makes the intrigue end with a bang, and hammers home the thesis. But from the point of view of Mrs. Alving's tragic quest as we have seen it develop through the rest of the play, this conclusion concludes nothing: it is merely sensational.

The exciting intrigue and the brilliantly, the violently clear surfaces of *Ghosts* are likely to obscure completely its real life and underlying form. The tragic rhythm, which Ibsen rediscovered by his long and loving attention to the reality of his fictive lives, is evident only to the histrionic sensibility. As Henry James put it, Ibsen's characters "have the extraordinary, the brilliant property of becoming when represented at once more abstract and more living": i.e., both their lives and the life of the play, the spiritual content and the form of the whole, are revealed in this medium. A Nazimova, a Duse, could show it to us on the stage. Lacking such a performance, the reader must endeavor to respond imaginatively and directly himself if he is to see the hidden poetry of *Ghosts*.

As Ibsen was fighting to present his poetic vision within the narrow theater admitted by modern realism, so his protagonist Mrs. Alving is fighting to realize her sense of human life in the blank photograph of her own stuffy parlor. She discovers there no means, no terms, and no nourishment; that is the truncated tragedy which underlies the savage thesis of the play. But she does find her son Oswald, and she makes of him the symbol of all she is seeking: freedom, innocence, joy, and truth. At the level of the life of the play, where Ibsen warms his characters into extraordinary human reality, they all have moral and emotional meanings for each other; and the pattern of their related actions, their partially blind struggle for the Alving

heritage, is consistent and very complex. In this structure, Mrs. Alving's changing relation to Oswald is only one strand, though an important one. I wish to consider it as a sample of Ibsen's rediscovery, through modern realism, of the tragic rhythm.

Oswald is of course not only a symbol for his mother, but a person in his own right, with his own quest for freedom and release, and his own anomalous stake in the Alving heritage. He is also a symbol for Pastor Manders of what he wants from Captain Alving's estate: the stability and continuity of the bourgeois conventions. In the economy of the play as a whole, Oswald is the hidden reality of the whole situation, like Oedipus' actual status as son-husband: the hidden fatality which, revealed in a series of tragic and ironic steps, brings the final peripety of the action. To see how this works, the reader is asked to consider Oswald's role in Act I and the beginning of Act II.

The main part of Act I (after a prologue between Regina and Engstrand) is a debate, or rather agon, between Mrs. Alving and the Pastor. The Pastor has come to settle the details of Mrs. Alving's bequest of her husband's money to the orphanage. They at once disagree about the purpose and handling of the bequest; and this disagreement soon broadens into the whole issue of Mrs. Alving's emancipation versus the Pastor's conventionality. The question of Oswald is at the center. The Pastor wants to think of him, and to make of him, a pillar of society such as the Captain was supposed to have been, while Mrs. Alving wants him to be her masterpiece of liberation. At this point Oswald himself wanders in, the actual but still mysterious truth underlying the dispute between his mother and the Pastor. His appearance produces what the Greeks would have called a complex recognition scene, with an implied peripety for both Mrs. Alving and the Pastor, which will not be realized by them until the end of the act. But this tragic development is written to be acted; it is to be found, not so much in the actual words of the characters, as in their moral-emotional responses and changing relationships to one another.

The Pastor has not seen Oswald since he grew up; and seeing him now he is startled as though by a real ghost; he recognizes him as the very reincarnation of his father: the same physique, the same mannerisms, even the same kind of pipe. Mrs. Alving with equal confidence recognizes him as her own son, and she notes that his mouth-mannerism is like the Pastor's. (She had been in love with the Pastor during the early years of her marriage, when she wanted to leave the Captain). As for Oswald himself, the mention of the pipe gives him a Proustian intermittence of the heart: he suddenly recalls a childhood scene when his father had given him his own pipe to smoke. He feels again the nausea and the cold sweat, and hears the Captain's hearty laughter. Thus in effect he recognizes himself as his father's, in the sense of his father's *victim;* a premonition of the ugly scene at the end of the play. But at this point no one is prepared to accept the full import of these insights. The whole scene is, on the surface, light and conventional, an accurate report of a passage of provincial politeness. Oswald wanders off for a walk before dinner, and the Pastor and his mother are left to bring their struggle more into the open.

Oswald's brief scene marks the end of the first round of the fight, and serves as prologue for the second round, much as the intervention of the chorus in the agon between Oedipus and Tiresias punctuates their struggle, and hints at an unexpected outcome on a new level of awareness. As soon as Oswald has gone, the Pastor launches an attack in form upon Mrs. Alving's entire emancipated way of life, with the question of Oswald, his role in the community, his upbringing and his future, always at the center of the attack. Mrs. Alving replies with her whole rebellious

philosophy, illustrated by a detailed account of her tormented life with the Captain, none of which the Pastor had known (or been willing to recognize) before. Mrs. Alving proves on the basis of this evidence that her new freedom is right; that her long secret rebellion was justified; and that she is now about to complete Oswald's emancipation, and thereby her own, from the swarming ghosts of the past. If the issue were merely on this rationalistic level, and between her and the Pastor, she would triumph at this point. But the real truth of her situation (as Oswald's appearance led us to suppose) does not fit either her rationalization or the Pastor's.

Oswald passes through the parlor again on his way to the dining room to get a drink before dinner, and his mother watches him in pride and pleasure. But from behind the door we hear the affected squealing of Regina. It is now Mrs. Alving's turn for an intermittence of the heart: it is as though she heard again her husband with Regina's mother. The insight which she had rejected before now reaches her in full strength, bringing the promised pathos and peripety; she sees Oswald, not as her masterpiece of liberation, but as the sinister, tyrannical, and continuing life of the past itself. The basis of her rationalization is gone; she suffers the breakdown of the moral being which she had built upon her now exploded view of Oswald.

At this point Ibsen brings down the curtain in obedience to the principles of the well-made play. The effect is to raise the suspense by stimulating our curiosity about the facts of the rest of the story. What will Mrs. Alving do now? What will the Pastor do—for Oswald and Regina are half-brother and sister; can we prevent the scandal from coming out? So the suspense is raised, but the attention of the audience is diverted from Mrs. Alving's tragic quest to the most literal, newspaper version of the facts.

The second act (which occurs immediately after dinner) is ostensibly concerned only with these gossipy facts. The Pastor and Mrs. Alving debate ways of handling the threatened scandal. But this is only the literal surface: Ibsen has his eye upon Mrs. Alving's shaken psyche, and the actual dramatic form of this scene, under the discussion which Mrs. Alving keeps up, is her pathos which the Act I curtain broke off. Mrs. Alving is suffering the blow in courage and faith; and she is rewarded with her deepest insight: "I am half inclined to think we are all ghosts, Mr. Manders. It is not only what we have inherited from our fathers and mothers that exists again in us, but all sorts of dead ideas and all kinds of old dead beliefs and things of that kind. They are not actually alive in us; but they are dormant all the same, and we can never be rid of them. Whenever I take up a newspaper and read it, I fancy I see ghosts creeping between the lines. There must be ghosts all over the world. They must be as countless as the grains of sand, it seems to me. And we are so miserably afraid of the light, all of us. This passage, in the fumbling phrases of Ibsen's provincial lady, and in William Archer's translation, is not by itself the poetry of the great dramatic poets. It does not have the verbal music of Racine, nor the freedom and sophistication of Hamlet, nor the scope of the Sophoclean chorus, with its use of the full complement of poetic and musical and theatrical resources. But in the total situation in the Alving parlor which Ibsen has so carefully established, and in terms of Mrs. Alving's uninstructed but profoundly developing awareness, it has its own hidden poetry: a poetry not of words but of the theater, a poetry of the histrionic sensibility. From the point of view of the underlying form of the play—the form as "the soul" of the tragedy—this scene completes the sequence which began with the debate in Act I: it is the pathos-and-epiphany following that agon.

It is evident, I think, that insofar as Ibsen was able to obey his realistic scruple, his need for the disinterested perception of human life beneath the clichés of custom and rationalization, he rediscovered the perennial basis of tragedy. The poetry of *Ghosts* is under the words, in the detail of action, where Ibsen accurately sensed the tragic rhythm of human life in a thousand small figures. And these little "movements of the psyche" are composed in a complex rhythm like music, a formal development sustained (beneath the sensational story and the angry thesis) until the very end. But the action is not completed: Mrs. Alving is left screaming with the raw impact of the calamity. The music is broken off, the dissonance unresolved—or, in more properly dramatic terms, the acceptance of the catastrophe, leading to the final vision or epiphany which should correspond to the insight Mrs. Alving gains in Act II, is lacking. The action of the play is neither completed nor placed in the wider context of meanings which the disinterested or contemplative purposes of poetry demand.

The unsatisfactory end of *Ghosts* may be understood in several ways. Thinking of the relation between Mrs. Alving and Oswald, one might say that she had romantically loaded more symbolic values upon her son than a human being can carry; hence his collapse proves too much—more than Mrs. Alving or the audience can digest. One may say that, at the end, Ibsen himself could not quite dissociate himself from his rebellious protagonist and see her action in the round, and so broke off in anger, losing his tragic vision in the satisfaction of reducing the bourgeois parlor to a nightmare, and proving the hollowness of a society which sees human life in such myopic and dishonest terms. As a thesis play, *Ghosts* is an ancestor of many related genres: Brieux's arguments for social reform, propaganda plays like those of the Marxists, or parables *à la* Andreev, or even Shaw's more generalized plays of the play-of-thought about social questions. But this use of the theater of modern realism for promoting or discussing political and social ideas never appealed to Ibsen. It did not solve his real problem, which was to use the publicly ac-

cepted theater of his time for poetic purposes. The most general way to understand
the unsatisfactory end of *Ghosts* is to say
that Ibsen could not find a way to represent
the action of his protagonist, with all its
moral and intellectual depth, within the
terms of modern realism. In the attempt he
truncated this action, and revealed as in a
brilliant light the limitations of the bourgeois parlor as the scene of human life.

Oswald is the chief symbol of what Mrs.
Alving is seeking, and his collapse ends her
quest in a horrifying catastrophe. But in
the complex life of the play, all of the persons and things acquire emotional and
moral significance for Mrs. Alving; and at
the end, to throw as much light as possible
upon the catastrophe, Ibsen brings all of the
elements of his composition together in
their highest symbolic valency. The orphanage has burned to the ground; the
Pastor has promised Engstrand money for
his "Sailor's Home" which he plans as a
brothel; Regina departs, to follow her
mother in the search for pleasure and money. In these eventualities the conventional
morality of the Alving heritage is revealed
as lewdness and dishonesty, quickly consumed in the fires of lust and greed, as Oswald himself (the central symbol) was
consumed even before his birth. But what
does this wreckage mean? Where are we to
place it in human experience? Ibsen can
only place it in the literal parlor, with lamp-
light giving place to daylight, and sunrise
on the empty, stimulating, virginal snow-
peaks out the window. The emotional force
of this complicated effect is very great; it
has the searching intimacy of nightmare.
But it is also as disquieting as a nightmare
from which we are suddenly awakened; it
is incomplete, and the contradiction between the inner power of dream and the
literal appearances of the daylight world is
unresolved. The spirit that moved Ibsen to
write the play, and which moved his protagonist through her tragic progress, is lost
to sight, disembodied, imperceptible in any

form unless the dreary exaltation of the in-
human mountain scene conveys it in feeling.

Henry James felt very acutely the contradiction between the deep and strict spirit
of Ibsen and his superb craftsmanship on
one side, and the little scene he tried to use
—the parlor in its surrounding void—on
the other. "If the spirit is a lamp within us,
glowing through what the world and the
flesh make of us as through a ground-glass
shade, then such pictures as Little Eyolf
and John Gabriel are each a chassez-croisez
of lamps burning, as in tasteless parlors,
with the flame practically exposed," he
wrote in *London Notes*.[1] "There is a positive odor of spiritual paraffin. The author
nevertheless arrives at the dramatist's great
goal—he arrives for all his meagerness at
intensity. The meagerness, which is after all
but an unconscious, an admirable economy,
never interferes with that: it plays straight
into the hands of his rare mastery of form.
The contrast between this form—so difficult to have reached, so 'evolved,' so civilized—and the bareness and bleakness of
his little northern democracy is the source
of half the hard frugal charm he puts
forth."

James had rejected very early in his career his own little northern democracy, that
of General Grant's America, with its ugly
parlor, its dead conventions, its enthusiastic
materialism, and its "non-conducting atmosphere." At the same time he shared Ibsen's ethical preoccupation, and his strict
sense of form. His comments on Ibsen are
at once the most sympathetic and the most
objective that have been written. But
James's own solution was to try to find a
better parlor for the theater of human life;
to present the quest of his American pil-
grim of culture on the wider "stage of Europe" as this might still be felt and suggested in the manners of the leisured classes
in England and France. James would have
nothing to do with the prophetic and revolutionary spirit which was driving the great

[1] Jan.–Aug., 1897.

continental authors, Ibsen among them. In his artistry and his moral exactitude Ibsen is akin to James; but this is not his whole story, and if one is to understand the spirit he tried to realize in Mrs. Alving, one must think of Kierkegaard, who had a great influence on Ibsen in the beginning of his career.

Kierkegaard (in *For Self-Examination*) has this to say of the disembodied and insatiable spirit of the times:

. . . thou wilt scarcely find anyone who does not believe in—let us say, for example, the spirit of the age, the *Zeitgeist*. Even he who has taken leave of higher things and is rendered blissful by mediocrity, yea, even he who toils slavishly for paltry ends or in the contemptible servitude of ill-gotten gains, even he believes, firmly and fully too, in the spirit of the age. Well, that is natural enough, it is by no means anything very lofty he believes in, for the spirit of the age is after all no higher than the age, it keeps close to the ground, so that it is the sort of spirit which it most like will-o'-the-wisp; but yet he believes in spirit. Or he believes in the world-spirit (*Weltgeist*) that strong spirit (for allurements, yes), that ingenious spirit (for deceits, yes); that spirit which Christianity calls an evil spirit—so that, in consideration of this, it is by no means anything very lofty he believes in when he believes in the world-spirit; but yet he believes in spirit. Or he believes in "the spirit of humanity," not spirit in the individual, but in the race, that spirit which, when it is god-forsaken for having forsaken God, is again, according to Christianity's teaching, an evil spirit—so that in view of this it is by no means anything very lofty he believes in when he believes in this spirit; but yet he believes in spirit.

On the other hand, as soon as the talk is about a holy spirit—how many, dost thou think, believe in it? Or when the talk is about an evil spirit which is to be renounced—how many, dost thou think, believe in such a thing? [2]

This description seems to me to throw some light upon Mrs. Alving's quest, upon Ibsen's modern-realistic scene, and upon the theater which his audience would accept. The other face of nineteenth century

[2] Kierkegaard, *For Self-Examination and Judge for Yourselves* (Princeton University Press, 1944), p. 94.

positivism is romantic aspiration. And Ibsen's realistic scene presents both of these aspects of the human condition: the photographically accurate parlor, in the foreground, satisfies the requirements of positivism, while the empty but stimulating scene out the window—Europe as a moral void, an uninhabited wilderness—offers as it were a blank check to the insatiate spirit. Ibsen always felt this exhilarating wilderness behind his cramped interiors. In *A Doll's House* we glimpse it as winter weather and black water. In *The Lady from the Sea* it is the cold ocean, with its whales and its gulls. In *The Wild Duck* it is the northern marshes, with wildfowl but no people. In the last scene of *Ghosts* it is, of course, the bright snow-peaks, which may mean Mrs. Alving's quest in its most disembodied and ambivalent form; very much the same sensuous moral void in which Wagner, having totally rejected the little human foreground where Ibsen fights his battles, unrolls the solitary action of passion. It is the "stage of Europe" before human exploration, as it might have appeared to the first hunters.

There is a kinship between the fearless and demanding spirit of Kierkegaard, and the spirit which Ibsen tried to realize in Mrs. Alving. But Mrs. Alving, like her contemporaries whom Kierkegaard describes, will not or cannot accept any interpretation of the spirit that drives her. It may look like the *Weltgeist* when she demands the joy of living, it may look like the Holy Ghost itself when one considers her appetite for truth. And it may look like the spirit of evil, a "goblin damned," when we see the desolation it produces. If one thinks of the symbols which Ibsen brings together in the last scene: the blank parlor, the wide unexplored world outside, the flames that consumed the Alving heritage and the sunrise flaming on the peaks, one may be reminded of the condition of Dante's great rebel Ulysses. He too is wrapped in the flame of his own consciousness, yet still dwells in the pride of the mind and the exhilaration of the world free of people, *il mondo senza gente*. But this analogy also may not be pressed too far. Ulysses is in hell; and when we explore the Mountain on which he was wrecked, we can place his condition with finality, and in relation to many other human modes of action and awareness. But Mrs. Alving's mountains do not place her anywhere: the realism of modern realism ends with the literal. Beyond that is not the ordered world of the tradition, but *Unendlichkeit*, and the anomalous "freedom" of undefined and uninformed aspiration.

Perhaps Mrs. Alving and Ibsen himself are closer to the role of Dante than to the role of Ulysses, seeing a hellish mode of being, but free to move on. Certainly Ibsen's development continued beyond *Ghosts*, and toward the end of his career he came much closer to achieving a consistent theatrical poetry within the confines of the theater of modern realism. He himself remarked that his poetry was to be found only in the series of his plays, no one of which was complete by itself.

M. C. Bradbrook

The Wild Duck

IN THE four plays which lie at the centre of his work—*The Wild Duck, The Sea Woman, Rosmersholm,* and *Hedda Gabler*—Ibsen is no longer the State Satirist, no longer the man the Ibsenites thought he was. In each of these plays, it is life—complex, delicate, and vulnerable—which he sets against systems of thought, however advanced and high-minded, and against merely intellectual convictions, however sincere. The advocates of the New Morality were ten years behind Ibsen, although they thought they had found their champion. But Ibsen had ceased to be polemical; the need for generosity and selflessness could not be hammered home with the concentrated fierceness appropriate to advocating intellectual honesty.

In these four plays, Ibsen is always for the complex as against the simple solution, for the scrupulous as against the doctrinaire mind. Gregers, Kroll and Tesman have in common the great failing which was for Ibsen the sin without forgiveness: too much of their mind works automatically. Their opinions have hardened and ossified, and cut them off from full experience of what happens to them. The disease takes a subtler form in them than in Helmer or Manders; in Tesman it is only the pedant's short-sightedness—which can entertain or even endear in the absent-minded professor. Yet how completely he is damned! the more completely because Ibsen allows him kindliness, disinterested friendship and humility which Helmer and Manders are denied. Ibsen's own intolerance and intellectual arrogance had mitigated. He no longer wanted to torpedo the Ark.

That these plays should have been distorted into a Programme of Reform is a final irony which could not have been lost on Ibsen himself. He gave up trying to explain them. He merely continued to write.

The subject of the plays is human relationships in the fullest sense. Not the strong situation, the meeting of "the fell incensèd point of mighty opposites," but the half-sensed, half-obliterated ties of ordinary life; the trusts, the stabilities, the adhesions of older, more settled modes of feeling. The characters—quite naturally, quite inevitably—are getting nearer to middle age. The method is becoming less theatrical, less explicit. The conscious discipline and control which make *A Doll's House* and *Ghosts* such obvious models for young writers—which evoked imitations such as Hauptmann's *Before Sunrise*—were replaced by a subtler and less conscious discipline, a control which was more indirect but more comprehensive. The last relics of the school of Scribe were disappearing also.

Hedda's game with the pistols is a very different use of conventional material from Nora's dancing of the tarantella. The pistols are consciously theatrical to herself and to the others, they are part of her "life-craving." The melodrama of the pistols is set against the background of Aunt Julle's domesticities and Tesman's solicitudes, and the implications are ironic. The four plays show indeed a progressive severity of control, until in *Hedda Gabler* the screw is turned so tightly that Ibsen has achieved the perfect specimen piece. Like *A Doll's House, Hedda Gabler* is so finished a production that it brought Ibsen himself to a

Reprinted with the permission of The Macmillan Company from *Ibsen the Norwegian* by M. C. Bradbrook. First published in 1946 by Chatto and Windus.

full stop, and he began again in a new way, whilst his disciples found it a model upon which they could base their own variations.

There is no answer to Hedda. Even the Ibsenites could not find a problem in this play.[1] But equally there is no answer to Rebekke or Rosmer, to Hjalmer, Gregers and Hedvig, and the answer to Ellida does not meet the deepest implications of her need. In an age which was always certain, even if it were only certain that no certainty existed, an age which was Rationalist in its scepticism and Positivist in its doubt, Ibsen saw, and not dogmatically but deliberately set it down, that the method of question and answer, of problem and solution, is no method for the artist.

The Wild Duck and *Rosmersholm* are the ripest of Ibsen's plays. *Peer Gynt* and *Bygmester Solness* may range wider and probe deeper, but here are his most masterful and most harmonious works. Vision and craftsmanship, power and skill are in equilibrium. These were not plays to be imitated by the disciples, for they depend on qualities in the writing that belong only to Ibsen himself.

Like *Hamlet*, *The Wild Duck* can be interpreted by each man in his own image. "The single vision" deepened and grew mysteriously active, mutable and various; the tide rises and falls, the light fades and gleams; to seek definitions is to go and catch a falling star. One day it will read as a tragedy, the next as the harshest irony; parts of it are clumsy, in other parts are embedded old controversies of that time. So searching yet so delicate is the touch, that these flaws and vagaries seem in themselves to strengthen the work. In this play and in *Rosmersholm* Ibsen perfected his own special power; the power to infuse the particular, drab, limited fact with a halo and a glory.

A room is to him a room, a writing table a writing table, and a waste paper basket, a waste paper basket [says Mrs. Woolf]. At the same time, the paraphernalia of reality have at certain moments to become the veil through which we see infinity. When Ibsen achieves this, as he certainly does, it is not by performing some miraculous conjuring trick at the critical moment. He achieves it by putting us into the right mood from the very start and by giving us the right materials for his purpose. He gives us the effect of ordinary life . . . but he gives it us by choosing a very few facts and those of a highly relevant kind. Thus when the moment of illumination comes, we accept it implicitly. We are neither roused nor puzzled; we do not have to ask ourselves, What does this mean? We simply feel that the thing we are looking at is lit up, and its depths revealed. It has not ceased to be itself by becoming something else. . . . The object which has been so uncompromisingly solid becomes, or should become, luminously transparent.[2]

Mrs. Woolf is describing a poet's power; it reads almost as a paraphrase of Wordsworth's aims in the preface to *Lyrical Ballads*. Ibsen had suppressed the poet in himself but this suppressed power lights up his writing, giving it not only the rich concentration of *A Doll's House*, but the unifying cohesion of the symbolic.

The rationalist students of Ibsen tried to pin a single meaning on to his symbols; was the wild duck symbolic of Hedvig or of Hjalmer or of Gregers? was Gregers a portrait of Ibsen or was he not? No one is likely to react in that way now. The photographer's studio, that most oddly particular and specific scene, and the attic which is the refuge of the maimed, the solitary and the defeated, with dusty trees and stopped clocks, and fragments of half a dozen smashed lives—these are the ocean depths that reflect infinity.

> *The Mind, that Ocean where each kind*
> *Does streight its own resemblance find;*
> *Yet it creates, transcending these,*
> *Far other Worlds and other Seas.*

The old lumber room was a childhood memory of Ibsen: he too had brooded over the old *History of London* "with the figures

---

[1] See the preface to Archer's translation in the *Collected Works* (Vol. X, p. xvii).

[2] *The Death of the Moth* (Hogarth, 1942), p. 108.

a pretty dart in turn. Miss Aurora Leigh— a notable social reformer—bids Lady Waldemar remember how

> You sold that poisonous porridge called your soul,

and, beside her invective, Greger's words to old Wehrle sound almost filial.[8] But the force of these scenes is almost entirely lost upon the reader of today.

In a sense, of course, Gregers is a permanent figure; he is the man who has found the entire solution to life in a creed, whether that of Marx or Freud, the Oxford Group or Yoga. He is Brand turned inside out. He sees his mother as right and his father as wrong. He feels wronged by his father, and at the same time morbidly conscious of a duty towards Hjalmer, so he is driven to interference. In none of his highminded attempts does he pay any attention to the delicate human material he is handling—being what Hedda Gabler called "a specialist." Nevertheless, Relling's brutalities are beside the mark. Gregers himself is mentally abnormal and, as he hints, physically a doomed man.

The play begins with his story; but the Ekdals run away with it. Ibsen said in a letter to his publisher, "The characters of *The Wild Duck* have endeared themselves to me," and by the characters, he clearly meant the Ekdals. Relling does his best to keep the play on a straight line with his sermon on the life-fantasy—in which he was anticipated by Francis Bacon;[9] but in the later acts Gregers is chiefly a "feed" to the Ekdals; he knits up an episode, or evokes a confidence from Hjalmer or Hedvig, but has little independent life.

The Ekdals gleam with vitality, even the

[8] *Aurora Leigh* was written by Mrs. Browning in 1857.
[9] "Doth any man doubt that if there were taken out of men's minds vain opinions, flattering hopes, false valuations, imaginations as one would, and the like, but it would leave the minds of a number of men poor shrunken things, full of melancholy and indisposition, and unpleasing to themselves." (*Essays: Of Truth.*)

sodden old Lieutenant. They are complex people who have simple minds. In the scene where old Ekdal decides to show Gregers the wild duck, they infect one another with excitement, until at last Hjalmer, who had begun by being rather ashamed of his hobby, joins in the chorus.

Lieut. Ekdal: That's where the rabbits go at night, old man!
Gregers: No, really? you've got rabbits too?
Lieut. Ekdal: Yes, you can well believe we've got rabbits. He's asking if we're got rabbits, Hjalmer! Aha! But now comes the great thing, look you! Now for it! Look out, Hedvig! Stand here: like that: now look in. Do you see a basket full of straw?
Gregers: Yes. And I see there's a bird in the basket.
Lieut. Ekdal: Aha—"a bird"!
Gregers: Isn't it a duck?
Lieut. Ekdal: Yes, you can bet it's a duck!
Hjalmer: But WHAT SORT of duck, do you think?
Hedvig: It's not an ordinary duck—
Lieut. Ekdal: Sh! Sh!

In this second act, the charm and absurdity of the Ekdals are enhanced by their innocent self-deceptions. The old man pretending he wants his hot water only for his ink, Hjalmer crying "No beer at a moment like this! Give me my flute!" are safe in the hands of their womenfolk, practising the ancient conspiratorial art of "managing father." What is humiliation for Nora becomes a game for Gina and Hedvig. It is a housecraft handed down from mother to daughter with the family recipes and ranging from maxims like "Feed the brute"— "Beer, father! lovely cool beer!" cries Hedvig—to that genuine faith in the Great Inventor which only the simple and childish could entertain, but which is the basis of Hjalmer's well-being. For he is a timid soul, easily snubbed, and needs the constant worship of his family to keep him in good heart. Hence his fretfulness at any suggestion of criticism; he feels betrayed from within the citadel.

Unsparingly as he is exposed, Hjalmer

is not condemned. He, too, had endeared himself to Ibsen. He is not a Pecksniff or even a Skimpole—rather is he a Micawber. When his preparation for heroic flight is punctured by Gina's "But what about all the rabbits?" he first cries despairingly, "What! have I got to take all the rabbits with me?" but almost at once wrests the alarming situation to his own advantage— "Father must get used to it. There are higher things than rabbits, which *I* have had to give up." His meanest act is when he gets Hedvig to finish his work so that he can potter in the attic, but salves his conscience by saying: "Don't hurt your eyes, do you hear? I'm not going to answer for it: you must decide for yourself, and so I warn you."

But his relish of the "patent contrivance" and his passionate concern about "a new path to the water-trough" are at least evidence of *livsglaeden* if not of *arbeitsglaeden*. He is so childish that he asks only for a part to play and an audience to applaud. Old Wehrle's cast-off mistress and her child are the perfect audience—docile, responsive, uncritical. His anger when he first suspects Hedvig not to be his is blind, savage and genuine.

Hjalmer: My home's in ruins! (Bursts into tears.) Gregers, I have no child now!
Hedvig: What's that? Father! Father!
Gina: Look at that, now!
Hjalmer: Don't come near me, Hedvig! Go away . . . I can't bear to see her. Ah . . . her eyes . . . Goodbye.
Hedvig (screams): No! No! Don't leave me!
Gina: Look at the child, Hjalmer! Look at the child!
Hjalmer: I won't! I can't! I'm going—away from all this.

But his later cruelty is false play-acting. "In these last minutes in my old home I wish to be free from—intruders!" "Does he mean me, mother?" asks Hedvig, trembling. In his last explanation to Gregers, Hjalmer admits his dependence on her love and hero-worship, a little too clearly to be completely in character. "There is that ter-

rible doubt—perhaps Hedvig never really loved me . . ." and he makes up a fantasy of how Hedvig had all the time been really laughing at him and deceiving him.[10] The appetite for proof of affection is begotten of anxiety, and in this confession, Hjalmer becomes pitiable, because he, too, is seen to be bankrupt, and broken. Selfish and parasitic as his love was, it sprang from and satisfied his deepest need.

Hjalmer is both a tragic and a comic figure: Hedvig, like Antigone and Cordelia, is the victim who redeems. She is a mere child, saying prayers for the wild duck "that it may be preserved from all harm," and making her deep-laid plans to keep father in good humour. But she is mysterious too: like the wild duck, no one knows "where she came from, or who her friends are"—it is essentially an open question whether she is Hjalmer's child or old Wehrle's; and she is subject to strange adolescent tides of feeling that rise "from the ocean depths." Hedvig's piteous limitations leave her exposed to catastrophe. She does believe in Hjalmer, as no one but a child could do. He is her God and when he betrays her, she is terror-stricken with all the final black despair of childhood. Gregers, in prompting her to kill the wild duck, uses the language of religion. It is to be a witness-bearing, a ritual sacrifice, to propitiate Hjalmer, the offended God. And so when Hjalmer presents his final "demand of the ideal"—"If I were to say, 'Hedvig, art willing to give up this *life* for me?'— thanks, you'd soon see the answer!" Hedvig puts the pistol to her own breast and fires. Yet it is unresolved whether she died in grief or as a sacrifice; from an adolescent impulse to self-destruction, or a childish desire for revenge—"I'll die and *then* you'll be sorry."

Her death is catastrophic, the only un-

[10] This is curiously enough the main theme of Helge Krog's play, *On Life's Sunny Side*, which was produced in 1944 by the Arts Theater in London. The husband's testing of his wife is very reminiscent of Gregers's test for Hedvig.

ambiguous event in the play; yet its causes are veiled. It is not related to the previous action by the kind of iron chain that draws on Osvald's death. It is a shock yet inevitable. Gina, gathering the remnants of her poor tenderness, speaks the last word: "The child mustn't lie out here to be looked at. She shall go in her own little room, my pet."

The most mysterious and potent symbol of all is not a human character but the wild duck itself. Each of the characters has something in common with the wild duck's story, but that story reflects all the scattered lights of the play and focuses them in one. The potency and power of the wild duck is that of the ghost in *Hamlet*, or the witches in *Macbeth:* it unites and concentrates the implications which lie behind the action of individuals.

Relling's final gibe at Gregers belongs to another world—the world of judgments, views and reason; the greatness of this play is that it moves upon so many levels simultaneously. Ibsen was no longer limited by his chosen technique. The freedom and scope of *The Wild Duck* are a symptom of that increasing depth of humanity and generosity which was taking Ibsen further and further from the doctrinal and the propagandist. "Dramatic categories," he observed, "are elastic and must accommodate themselves to literary fact." The characters had endeared themselves to him and the dramatic category was modified accordingly, so that even the weakest is allowed to hint that he too has known "the ocean's depths."

Henry James

On the Occasion of *Hedda Gabler*

WHETHER or no Henrik Ibsen be a master of his art, he has had a fortune that, in the English-speaking world, falls not always even to the masters—the fortune not only of finding himself the theme of many pens and tongues, but the rarer privilege and honour of acting as a sort of register of the critical atmosphere, a barometer of the intellectual weather. Interesting or not in himself (the word on this point varies from the fullest affirmation to the richest denial), he has sounded in our literary life a singularly interesting hour. At any rate he himself constitutes an episode, an event, if the sign of such action be to have left appearances other than you found them. He has cleared up the air we breathe and set a copy to our renouncement; has made many things wonderfully plain and quite mapped out the prospect. Whenever such service is rendered, the attentive spirit is the gainer; these are its moments of amplest exercise. Illusions are sweet to the dreamer, but not so to the observer, who has a horror of a fool's paradise. Henrik Ibsen will have led him inexorably into the rougher road. Such recording and illuminating agents are precious; they tell us where we are in the thickening fog of life, and we feel for them much of the grateful respect excited in us at sea, in dim weather, by the exhibition of the mysterious instrument with which the captain takes an observation. We have held *Ghosts*, or *Rosmersholm*, or *Hedda Gabler* in our hand, and *they* have been our little instrument—they have enabled us to emulate the wary mariner; the consequence of which is that we know at least on what shores we may ground or in what ports we may anchor. The author of these strange works has in short performed a function which was doubtless no part of his purpose. This was to tell us about his own people; yet what has primarily happened is that he has brought about an exhibition of ours.

It is a truly remarkable show, for as to where *nous en sommes*, as the phrase goes, in the art of criticism and the movement of curiosity, as to our accumulations of experience and our pliancy of intelligence, our maturity of judgement and our distinction of tone, our quick perception of quality and (peculiar glory of our race) our fine feeling for shades, he has been the means of our acquiring the most copious information. Whether or no we may say that as a sequel to this we know Dr. Ibsen better, we may at least say that we know more about ourselves. We glow with the sense of how we may definitely look to each other to take things, and that is an immense boon, representing in advance a wonderful economy of time, a saving of useless effort and vain appeal. The great clarifying fact has been that, with *Hedda Gabler* and *Ghosts* and all the rest, we have stood in an exceptionally agitated way in the presence of the work of art, and have gained thereby a peculiarly acute consciousness of how we tend to consider it. It has been interesting to perceive that we consider the work of art with passion, with something approaching to fury. Under its influence we sweep the whole keyboard of emotion, from frantic enjoyment to ineffable disgust. Resentment and reprobation happen to have been

Reprinted from *The Scenic Art*, ed. Allan Wade, Rutgers University Press, New Brunswick, N.J., and Rupert Hart-Davis, London, 1948. First published in the *New Review*, June, 1891. Reprinted by permission.

indeed in the case before us the notes most frequently sounded; but this is obviously an accident, not impairing the value of the illustration, the essence of which is that our critical temper remains exactly the *naïf* critical temper, the temper of the spectators in the gallery of the theatre who howl at the villain of the play.

It has been the degree in general, of the agitation that has been remarkable in the case before us, as may conveniently be gathered from a glance at the invaluable catalogue of denouncements drawn up by Mr. William Archer after perusal of the articles lately dedicated by the principal London journals to a couple of representations of Ibsen; that, if I mistake not, of *Ghosts* and that of *Rosmersholm*. This catalogue is a precious document, one of those things that the attentive spirit would not willingly let die. It is a thing, at any rate, to be kept long under one's hand, as a mine of suggestion and reference; for it illuminates, in this matter of the study of Ibsen, the second characteristic of our emotion (the first as I have mentioned, being its peculiar intensity): the fact that that emotion is conspicuously and exclusively moral, one of those cries of outraged purity which have so often and so pathetically resounded through the Anglo-Saxon world.

We have studied our author, it must be admitted, under difficulties, for it is impossible to read him without perceiving that merely book in hand we but half know him—he addresses himself so substantially to representation. This quickens immensely our consideration for him, since in proportion as we become conscious that he has mastered an exceedingly difficult form are we naturally reluctant, in honour, to judge him unaccompanied by its advantages, by the benefit of his full intention. Considering how much Ibsen has been talked about in England and America, he has been lamentably little seen and heard. Until *Hedda Gabler* was produced in London six weeks ago, there had been but one attempt to represent its predecessors that had consisted

of more than a single performance. This circumstance has given a real importance to the undertaking of the two courageous young actresses who have brought the most recent of the author's productions to the light and who have promptly found themselves justified in their talent as well as in their energy. It was a proof of Ibsen's force that he had made us chatter about him so profusely without the aid of the theatre; but it was even more a blessing to have the aid at last. The stage is to the prose drama (and Ibsen's later manner is the very prose of prose) what the tune is to the song or the concrete case to the general law. It immediately becomes apparent that he needs the test to show his strength and the frame to show his picture. An extraordinary process of vivification takes place; the conditions seem essentially enlarged. Those of the stage in general strike us for the most part as small enough, so that the game played in them is often not more inspiring than a successful sack-race. But Ibsen reminds us that if they do not in themselves confer life they can at least receive it when the infusion is artfully attempted. Yet how much of it they were doomed to receive from *Hedda Gabler* was not to be divined till we had seen *Hedda Gabler* in the frame. The play, on perusal, left one comparatively muddled and mystified, fascinated, but—in one's intellectual sympathy—snubbed. Acted, it leads that sympathy over the straightest of roads with all the exhilaration of a superior pace. Much more, I confess, one doesn't get from it; but an hour of refreshing exercise is a reward in itself. The sense of being moved by a scientific hand as one sits in one's stall has not been spoiled for us by satiety.

Hedda Gabler then, in the frame, is exceedingly vivid and curious, and a part of its interest is in the way it lights up in general the talent of the author. It is doubtless not the most complete of Ibsen's plays, for it owes less to its subject than to its form; but it makes good his title to the possession of a real method, and in thus

putting him before us as a master it ex-
hibits at the same time his irritating, his
bewildering incongruities. He is nothing, as
a literary personality, if not positive; yet
there are moments when his great gift
seems made up of negatives, or at any rate
when the total seems a contradiction of
each of the parts. I premise of course that
we hear him through a medium not his
own, and I remember that translation is a
shameless falsification of colour. Translation, however, is probably not wholly re-
sponsible for three appearances inherent in
all his prose work, as we possess it, though
in slightly differing degrees, and yet quite
unavailing to destroy in it the expression of
life; I mean of course the absence of
humour, the absence of free imagination,
and the absence of style. The absence of
style, both in the usual and in the larger
sense of the word, is extraordinary, and
all the more mystifying that its place is not
usurped, as it frequently is in such cases,
by vulgarity. Ibsen is massively common
and "middle-class," but neither his spirit
nor his manner is small. He is never trivial
and never cheap, but he is in nothing more
curious than in owing to a single source
such distinction as he retains. His people
are of inexpressive race; they give us essentially the *bourgeois* impression; even when
they are furiously nervous and, like Hedda,
more than sufficiently fastidious, we recognise that they live, with their remarkable
creator, in a world in which selection has
no great range. This is perhaps one reason
why they none of them, neither the creator
nor the creatures, appear to feel much impulse to *play* with the things of life. This
impulse, when it breaks out, is humour, and
in the scenic genius it usually breaks out in
one place or another. We get the feeling, in
Ibsen's plays, that such whims are too ultimate, too much a matter of luxury and
leisure for the stage of feeling at which his
characters have arrived. They are all too
busy learning to live—humour will come in
later, when they know how. A certain angular irony they frequently manifest, and

some of his portraits are strongly satirical,
like that, to give only two instances, of
Tesman, in *Hedda Gabler* (a play indeed
suffused with irrepressible irony), or that
of Hialmar Ekdal, in *The Wild Duck*. But it
is the ridicule without the smile, the dance
without the music, a sort of sarcasm that
is nearer to tears than to laughter. There
is nothing very droll in the world, I think,
to Dr. Ibsen; and nothing is more interesting than to see how he makes up his world
without a joke. Innumerable are the vic-
tories of talent, and art is a legerdemain.

It is always difficult to give an example
of an absent quality, and, if the romantic
is even less present in Ibsen than the comic,
this is best proved by the fact that everything seems to us inveterately observed.
Nothing is more puzzling to the readers of
his later work than the reminder that he
is the great dramatic poet of his country,
or that the author of *The Pillars of Society*
is also the author of *Brand* and *Peer Gynt,*
compositions which, we are assured, testify
to an audacious imagination and abound in
complicated fantasy. In his satiric studies
of contemporary life, the impression that is
strongest with us is that the picture is infinitely *noted,* that all the patience of the
constructive pessimist is in his love of the
detail of character and of conduct, in his
way of accumulating the touches that illustrate them. His recurrent ugliness of surface, as it were, is a sort of proof of his
fidelity to the real, in a spare, strenuous,
democratic community; just as the same
peculiarity is one of the sources of his
charmless fascination—a touching vision of
strong forces struggling with a poverty, a
bare provinciality, of life. I call the fascination of Ibsen charmless (for those who feel
it at all), because he holds us without brib-
ing us; he squeezes the attention till he
almost hurts it, yet with never a concilia-
tory stroke. He has as little as possible to
say to our taste; even his large, strong form
takes no account of that, gratifying it without concessions. It is the oddity of the
mixture that makes him so individual—his

perfect practice of a difficult and delicate art, combined with such aesthetic density. Even in such a piece as *The Lady from the Sea* (much the weakest, to my sense, of the whole series), in which he comes nearer than in others—unless indeed it be in *Hedda Gabler*—to playing with an idea from the simple instinct of sport, nothing could be less picturesque than the general effect, with every inherent incentive to have made it picturesque. The idea might have sprung from the fancy of Hawthorne, but the atmosphere is the hard light of Ibsen. One feels that the subject should have been tinted and distanced; but, in fact, one has to make an atmosphere as one reads and one winces considerably under "Doctor Wangel" and the pert daughters.

For readers without curiosity as to their author's point of view (and it is doubtless not a crime not to have it, though I think it is a misfortune, an open window the less), there is too much of "Doctor Wangel" in Ibsen altogether—using the good gentleman's name for what it generally represents or connotes. It represents the ugly interior on which his curtain inexorably rises and which, to be honest, I like for the queer associations it has taught us to respect: the hideous carpet and wall-paper and curtains (one may answer for them), the conspicuous stove, the lonely centre-table, the "lamps with green shades," as in the sumptuous first act of *The Wild Duck*, the pervasive air of small interests and standards, the sign of limited local life. It represents the very clothes, the inferior fashions, of the figures that move before us, and the shape of their hats and the tone of their conversation and the nature of their diet. But the oddest thing happens in connection with this effect—the oddest extension of sympathy or relaxation of prejudice. What happens is that we feel that whereas, if Ibsen were weak or stupid or vulgar, this parochial or suburban stamp would only be a stick to beat him with, it acts, as the case stands, and in the light of his singular masculinity, as a sort of sub-

stitute—a little clumsy, if you like—for charm. In a word, it becomes touching, so that practically the *blasé* critical mind enjoys it as a refinement. What occurs is very analogous to what occurs in our appreciation of the dramatist's remarkable art, his admirable talent for producing an intensity of interest by means incorruptibly quiet, by that almost demure preservation of the appearance of the usual in which we see him juggle with difficulty and danger and which constitutes, as it were, his only coquetry. There are people who are indifferent to these mild prodigies; there are others for whom they will always remain the most charming privilege of art.

Hedda Gabler is doubtless as suburban as any of its companions; which is indeed a fortunate circumstance, inasmuch as if it were less so we should be deprived of a singularly complete instance of a phenomenon difficult to express, but which may perhaps be described as the operation of talent without glamour. There is notoriously no glamour over the suburbs, and yet nothing could be more vivid than Dr. Ibsen's account of the incalculable young woman into whom Miss Robins so artistically projects herself. To "like" the play, as we phrase it, is doubtless therefore to give one of the fullest examples of our constitutional inability to control our affections. Several of the spectators who have liked it most will probably admit even that, with themselves, this sentiment has preceded a complete comprehension. They would perhaps have liked it better if they had understood it better—as to this they are not sure; but they at any rate liked it well enough. Well enough for what? the question may of course always be in such a case. To be absorbed, assuredly, which is the highest tribute we can pay to any picture of life, and a higher one than most pictures attempted succeed in making us pay. Ibsen is various, and *Hedda Gabler* is probably an ironical pleasantry, the artistic exercise of a mind saturated with the vision of human infirmities; saturated, above all, with a sense of the infinitude, for all its mortal savour, of *character,* finding that an endless romance and a perpetual challenge. Can there have been at the source of such a production a mere refinement of conscious power, an enjoyment of difficulty and a preconceived victory over it? We are free to imagine that in this case Dr. Ibsen chose one of the last subjects that an expert might have been expected to choose, for the harmless pleasure of feeling and of showing that he was in possession of a method that could make up for its deficiencies.

The demonstration is complete and triumphant, but it does not conceal from us— on the contrary—that his drama is essentially that supposedly undramatic thing, the picture not of an action but of a condition. It is the portrait of a nature, the story of what Paul Bourget would call an *état d'âme,* and of a state of nerves as well as of soul, a state of temper, of health, of chagrin, of despair. *Hedda Gabler* is, in short, the study of an exasperated woman; and it may certainly be declared that the subject was not in advance, as a theme for scenic treatment, to be pronounced promising. There could in fact, however, be no more suggestive illustration of the folly of quarrelling with an artist over his subject. Ibsen has had only to take hold of this one in earnest to make it, against every presumption, live with an intensity of life. One can doubtless imagine other ways, but it is enough to say of this one that, put to the test, it imposes its particular spectacle. Something might have been gained, entailing perhaps a loss in another direction, by tracing the preliminary stages, showing the steps in Mrs. Tesman's history which led to the spasm, as it were, on which the curtain rises and of which the breathless duration— ending in death—is the period of the piece. But a play is above everything a work of selection, and Ibsen, with his curious and beautiful passion for the unity of time (carried in him to a point which almost always implies also that of place), condemns himself to admirable rigours. We receive Hedda ripe for her catastrophe, and if we ask for antecedents and explanations we must simply find them in her character. Her motives are just her passions. What the four acts show us is these motives and that character—complicated, strange, irreconcilable, infernal—playing themselves out. We know too little why she married Tesman, we see too little why she ruins Lövborg; but we recognise that she is infinitely perverse, and Heaven knows that, as the drama mostly goes, the crevices we are called upon to stop are singularly few. That Mrs. Tesman is a perfectly ill-regulated person is a matter of course, and there are doubtless spectators who would fain ask whether it would not have been better to represent in her stead a person totally different. The answer to this sagacious question seems to me to be simply that no one can possibly tell. There are many things in the world that are past finding out, and one of them is whether the subject of a work had not better have been another subject. We shall always do well to leave that matter to the author (*he* may have some secret for solving the riddle); so terrible would his revenge easily become if we were to accept a responsibility for his theme.

The distinguished thing is the firm hand that weaves the web, the deep and ingenious use made of the material. What material, indeed, the dissentient spirit may exclaim, and what "use," worthy of the sacred name, is to be made of a wicked, diseased, disagreeable woman? That is just what Ibsen attempts to gauge, and from the moment such an attempt is resolute the case ceases to be so simple. The "use" of Hedda Gabler is that she acts on others and that even her most disagreeable qualities have the privilege, thoroughly undeserved doubtless, but equally irresistible, of becoming a part of the history of others. And then one isn't so sure she is wicked, and by no means sure (especially when she is represented by an actress who makes the point ambiguous) that she is disagreeable. She is various and sinuous and graceful, complicated and natural; she suffers, she struggles, she is human, and by that fact exposed to a dozen interpretations, to the importunity of our suspense. Wrought with admirable closeness is the whole tissue of relations between the five people whom the author sets in motion and on whose behalf he asks of us so few concessions. That is for the most part the accomplished thing in Ibsen, the thing that converts his provincialism into artistic urbanity. He puts *us* to no expense worth speaking of—he takes all the expense himself. I mean that he thinks out our entertainment for us and shapes it of thinkable things, the passions, the idiosyncrasies, the cupidities and jealousies, the strivings and struggles, the joys and sufferings of men. The spectator's situation is different enough when what is given him is the mere dead rattle of the surface of life, into which *he* has to inject the element of thought, the "human interest." Ibsen kneads the soul of man like a paste, and often with a rude and indelicate hand to which the soul of man objects. Such a production as *The Pillars of Society*, with its large, dense complexity of moral cross-references and its admirable definiteness as a picture of motive and temperament (the whole canvas charged, as it were, with moral colour), such a production asks the average moral man to see too many things at once. It will never help Ibsen with the multitude that the multitude shall feel that the more they look the more intentions they shall see, for of such seeing of many intentions the multitude is but scantily desirous. It keeps indeed a positively alarmed and jealous watch in that direction; it smugly insists that intentions shall be rigidly limited.

This sufficiently answers the artless question of whether it may be hoped for the author of *The Pillars of Society* that he shall acquire popularity in this country. In what country under heaven might it have been hoped for him, or for the particular community, that he *should* acquire popularity? Is he in point of fact so established

and cherished in the Norwegian theatre? Do his countrymen understand him and clamour for him and love him, or do they content themselves—a very different affair —with being proud of him when aliens abuse him? The rumour reaches us that *Hedda Gabler* has found no favour at Copenhagen, where we are compelled to infer that the play had not the happy interpretation it enjoys in London. It would doubtless have been in danger here if tact and sympathy had not interposed. We hear that it has had reverses in Germany, where of late years Ibsen has been the fashion; but, indeed, all these are matters of an order as to which we should have been grateful for more information from those who have lately had the care of introducing the formidable dramatist to the English and American public. He excites, for example, in each case, all sorts of curiosity and conjecture as to the quality and capacity of the theatre to which, originally, such a large order was addressed: we are full of unanswered questions about the audience and the school.

What, however, has most of all come out in our timid and desultory experiments is that the author of *The Pillars of Society*, and of *The Doll's House*, of *Ghosts*, of *The Wild Duck*, of *Hedda Gabler*, is destined to be adored by the "profession." Even in his comfortless borrowed habit he will remain intensely dear to the actor and the actress. He cuts them out work to which the artistic nature in them joyously responds—work difficult and interesting, full of stuff and opportunity. The opportunity that he gives them is almost always to do the deep and delicate thing—the sort of chance that, in proportion as they are intelligent, they are most on the lookout for. He asks them to paint with a fine brush; for the subject that he gives them is ever our plastic humanity. This will surely preserve him (leaving out the question of serious competition) after our little flurry is over. It was what made the recent representation of *Hedda Gabler* so singularly interesting and refreshing. It was what gives importance to the inquiry as to how his call for "subtlety" in his interpreters has been met in his own country. It was impossible the other day not to be conscious of a certain envy (as of a case of artistic happiness) of the representatives of the mismated Tesmans and their companions—so completely, as the phrase is, were they "in" it and under the charm of what they had to do. In fact the series of Ibsen's "social dramas" is a dazzling array of parts. Nora Helmer will be undertaken again and again—of a morning, no doubt, as supposedly, though oddly, the more "earnest" hour—by young artists justly infatuated. The temptation is still greater to women than to men, as we feel in thinking, further, of the Rebecca of *Rosmersholm*, of Lona Hessel and Martha Bernick in the shapely *Pillars*, of the passionate mother and the insolent maid in the extraordinarily compact and vivid *Ghosts* —absurd and fascinating work; of Mrs. Linden, so quietly tragic, so tremulously real, in *The Doll's House*, and of that irresistibly touching image, so untainted with cheap pathos, Hedvig Ekdal, the little girl with failing eyes, in *The Wild Duck*, who pores over her story-book in the paltry photographic studio of her intensely humbugging father. Such a figure as this very Hialmar Ekdal, however, the seedy, selfish —subtly selfish and self-deceptive—photographer, in whom nothing is active but the tongue, testifies for the strong masculine side of the list. If *The League of Youth* is more nearly a complete comedy than any other of Ibsen's prose works, the comedian who should attempt to render Stensgard in that play would have a real portrait to reproduce. But the examples are numerous: Bernick and Rosmer, Oswald and Manders (Ibsen's compunctious "pastors" are admirable), Gregers Werle, the transcendent meddler in *The Wild Duck*, Rörlund, the prudish rector in the *Pillars*, Stockmann and the Burgomaster in *The Enemy of the People*, all stand, humanly and pictorially, on their feet.

This it is that brings us back to the author's great quality, the quality that makes him so interesting in spite of his limitations, so rich in spite of his lapses—his habit of dealing essentially with the individual caught in the fact. Sometimes, no doubt, he leans too far on that side, loses sight too much of the type-quality and gives his spectators free play to say that even caught in the fact his individuals are mad. We are not at all sure, for instance, of the type-quality in Hedda. Sometimes he makes so queer a mistake as to treat a pretty motive, like that of *The Lady from the Sea*, in a poor and prosaic way. He exposes himself with complacent, with irritating indifference to the objector as well as to the scoffer, he makes his "heredity" too short and his consequences too long, he deals with a homely and unaesthetic society, he harps on the string of conduct, and he actually talks of stockings and legs, in addition to other improprieties. He is not pleasant enough nor light enough nor casual enough; he is too far from Piccadilly and our glorious standards. Therefore his cause may be said to be lost; we shall never take him to our hearts. It was never to have been expected, indeed, that we should, for in literature religions usually grow their own gods, and *our* heaven—as every one can see—is already crowded. But for those who care in general for the form that he has practised he will always remain one of the talents that have understood it best and extracted most from it, have effected most neatly the ticklish transfusion of life. If we possessed the unattainable, an eclectic, artistic, disinterested theatre, to which we might look for alternation and variety, it would simply be a point of honour in such a temple to sacrifice sometimes to Henrik Ibsen.

James Joyce

When We Dead Awaken

TWENTY years have passed since Henrik Ibsen wrote *A Doll's House*, thereby almost marking an epoch in the history of drama. During those years his name has gone abroad through the length and breadth of two continents, and has provoked more discussion and criticism than that of any other living man. He has been upheld as a religious reformer, a social reformer, a Semitic lover of righteousness, and as a great dramatist. He has been rigorously denounced as a meddlesome intruder, a defective artist, an incomprehensible mystic, and, in the eloquent words of a certain English critic, "a muck-ferreting dog." Through the perplexities of such diverse criticism, the great genius of the man is day by day coming out as a hero comes out amid the earthly trials. The dissonant cries are fainter and more distant, the random praises are rising in steadier and more choral chaunt. Even to the uninterested bystander it must seem significant that the interest attached to this Norwegian has never flagged for over a quarter of a century. It may be questioned whether any man has held so firm an empire over the thinking world in modern times. Not Rousseau; not Emerson; not Carlyle; not any of those giants of whom almost all have passed out of human ken. Ibsen's power over two generations has been enhanced by his own reticence. Seldom, if at all, has he condescended to join battle with his enemies. It would appear as if the storm of fierce debate rarely broke in upon his wonderful calm. The conflicting voices have not influenced his work in the very smallest degree. His output of dramas has been regulated by the utmost order, by a clockwork routine, seldom found in the case of genius. Only once he answered his assailants after their violent attack on *Ghosts*. But from *The Wild Duck* to *John Gabriel Borkman*, his dramas have appeared almost mechanically at intervals of two years. One is apt to overlook the sustained energy which such a plan of campaign demands; but even surprise at this must give way to admiration at the gradual, irresistible advance of this extraordinary man. Eleven plays, all dealing with modern life, have been published. Here is the list: *A Doll's House, Ghosts, An Enemy of the People, The Wild Duck, Rosmersholm, The Lady from the Sea, Hedda Gabler, The Master Builder, Little Eyolf, John Gabriel Borkman*, and lastly— his new drama, published at Copenhagen, December 19th, 1899—*When We Dead Awaken*. This play is already in process of translation into almost a dozen different languages—a fact which speaks volumes for the power of its author. The drama is written in prose, and is in three acts.

To begin an account of a play of Ibsen's is surely no easy matter. The subject is, in one way, so confined, and, in another way, so vast. It is safe to predict that nine-tenths of the notices of this play will open in some such way as the following: "Arnold Rubek and his wife, Maja, have been married for four years, at the beginning of the play. Their union is, however, unhappy. Each is discontented with the other." So far as this goes, it is unimpeachable; but then it does not go very far. It does not convey even the

From *The Critical Essays of James Joyce*, ed. R. Ellmann and E. Mason, Faber and Faber, London, 1959; reprinted with the permission of the Society of Authors as the literary representative of the Estate of the late James Joyce. First published in the *Fortnightly Review* in 1900.

most shadowy notion of the relations between Professor Rubek and his wife. It is
a bald, clerkly version of countless, indefinable complexities. It is as though the
history of a tragic life were to be written
down rudely in two columns, one for the
pros and the other for the cons. It is only
saying what is literally true, to say that, in
the three acts of the drama, there has been
stated all that is essential to the drama.
There is from first to last hardly a superfluous word or phrase. Therefore, the play
itself expresses its own ideas as briefly and
as concisely as they can be expressed in
the dramatic form. It is manifest, then, that
a notice cannot give an adequate notion of
the drama. This is not the case with the
common lot of plays, to which the fullest
justice may be meted out in a very limited
number of lines. They are for the most part
reheated dishes—unoriginal compositions,
cheerfully owlish as to heroic insight, living
only in their own candid claptrap—in a
word, stagey. The most perfunctory curt-
ness is their fittest meed. But in dealing
with the work of a man like Ibsen, the task
set the reviewer is truly great enough to
sink all his courage. All he can hope to do is
to link some of the more salient points together in such a way as to suggest rather
than to indicate, the intricacies of the plot.
Ibsen has attained ere this to such mastery
over his art that, with apparently easy
dialogue, he presents his men and women
passing through different soul-crises. His
analytic method is thus made use of to the
fullest extent, and into the comparatively
short space of two days the life in life of
all his characters is compressed. For instance, though we only see Solness during
one night and up to the following evening,
we have in reality watched with bated
breath the whole course of his life up to the
moment when Hilda Wangel enters his
house. So in the play under consideration,
when we see Professor Rubek first, he is
sitting in a garden chair, reading his morning paper, but by degrees the whole scroll
of his life is unrolled before us, and we

have the pleasure not of hearing it read out
to us, but of reading it for ourselves, piec-
ing the various parts, and going closer to
see wherever the writing on the parchment
is fainter or less legible. . . .

Ibsen's plays do not depend for their interest on the action, or on the incidents.
Even the characters, faultlessly drawn
though they be, are not the first thing in
his plays. But the naked drama—either the
perception of a great truth, or the opening
up of a great question, or a great conflict
which is almost independent of the conflicting actors, and has been and is of far-
reaching importance—this is what primarily rivets our attention. Ibsen has chosen
the average lives in their uncompromising
truth for the groundwork of all his later
plays. He has abandoned the verse form,
and has never sought to embellish his work
after the conventional fashion. Even when
his dramatic theme reached its zenith he has
not sought to trick it out in gawds or
tawdriness. How easy it would have been to
have written *An Enemy of the People* on a
speciously loftier level—to have replaced
the *bourgeois* by the legitimate hero! Critics
might then have extolled as grand what they
have so often condemned as banal. But the
surroundings are nothing to Ibsen. The
play is the thing. By the force of his genius,
and the indisputable skill which he brings
to all his efforts, Ibsen has, for many years,
engrossed the attention of the civilized
world. Many years more, however, must
pass before he will enter his kingdom in
jubilation, although, as he stands to-day,
all has been done on his part to ensure his
own worthiness to enter therein. I do not
propose here to examine into every detail
of dramaturgy connected with this play, but
merely to outline the characterization.

In his characters Ibsen does not repeat
himself. In this drama—the last of a long
catalogue—he has drawn and differentiated
with his customary skill. What a novel
creation is Ulfheim! Surely the hand which
has drawn him has not yet lost her cunning.
Ulfheim is, I think, the newest character in

the play. He is a kind of surprise-packet. It is as a result of his novelty that he seems to leap, at first mention, into bodily form. He is superbly wild, primitively impressive. His fierce eyes roll and glare as those of Yégof or Herne. As for Lars, we may dismiss him, for he never opens his mouth. The Sister of Mercy speaks only once in the play, but then with good effect. In silence she follows Irene like a retribution, a voiceless shadow with her own symbolic majesty.

Irene, too, is worthy of her place in the gallery of her compeers. Ibsen's knowledge of humanity is nowhere more obvious than in his portrayal of women. He amazes one by his painful introspection; he seems to know them better than they know themselves. Indeed, if one may say so of an eminently virile man, there is a curious admixture of the woman in his nature. His marvellous accuracy, his faint traces of femininity, his delicacy of swift touch, are perhaps attributable to this admixture. But that he knows women is an incontrovertible fact. He appears to have sounded them to almost unfathomable depths. Beside his portraits the psychological studies of Hardy and Turgénieff, or the exhaustive elaborations of Meredith, seem no more than sciolism. With a deft stroke, in a phrase, in a word, he does what costs them chapters, and does it better. Irene, then, has to face great comparison; but it must be acknowledged that she comes forth of it bravely. Although Ibsen's women are uniformly true, they, of course, present themselves in various lights. Thus Gina Ekdal is, before all else, a comic figure, and Hedda Gabler a tragic one—if such old-world terms may be employed without incongruity. But Irene cannot be so readily classified; the very aloofness from passion, which is not separable from her, forbids classification. She interests us strangely—magnetically, because of her inner power of character. However perfect Ibsen's former creations may be, it is questionable whether any of his women reach to the depth of soul of Irene. She holds our gaze for the

sheer force of her intellectual capacity. She is, moreover, an intensely spiritual creation—in the truest and widest sense of that. At times she is liable to get beyond us, to soar above us, as she does with Rubek. It will be considered by some as a blemish that she—a woman of fine spirituality—is made an artist's model, and some may even regret that such an episode mars the harmony of the drama. I cannot altogether see the force of this contention; it seems pure irrelevancy. But whatever may be thought of the fact, there is small room for complaint as to the handling of it. Ibsen treats it, as indeed he treats all things, with large insight, artistic restraint, and sympathy. He sees it steadily and whole, as from a great height, with perfect vision and an angelic dispassionateness, with the sight of one who may look on the sun with open eyes. Ibsen is different from the clever purveyor.

Maja fulfills a certain technical function in the play, apart from her individual character. Into the sustained tension she comes as a relief. Her airy freshness is as a breath of keen air. The sense of free, almost flamboyant, life, which is her chief note, counterbalances the austerity of Irene and the dullness of Rubek. Maja has practically the same effect on this play, as Hilda Wangel has on *The Master Builder*. But she does not capture our sympathy so much as Nora Helmer. She is not meant to capture it.

Rubek himself is the chief figure in this drama, and, strangely enough, the most conventional. Certainly, when contrasted with his Napoleonic predecessor, John Gabriel Borkman, he is a mere shadow. It must be borne in mind, however, that Borkman is alive, actively, energetically, restlessly alive, all through the play to the end, when he dies; whereas Arnold Rubek is dead, almost hopelessly dead, until the end, when he comes to life. Notwithstanding this, he is supremely interesting, not because of himself, but because of his dramatic significance. Ibsen's drama, as I have said, is wholly independent of his characters. They may be bores, but the drama in which they live and move is invariably powerful. Not that Rubek is a bore by any means! He is infinitely more interesting in himself than Torvald Helmer or Tesman, both of whom possess certain strongly-marked characteristics. Arnold Rubek is, on the other hand, not intended to be a genius, as perhaps Eljert Lövborg is. Had he been a genius like Eljert he would have understood in a truer way the value of his life. But, as we are to suppose, the facts that he is devoted to his art and that he has attained to a degree of mastery in it—mastery of hand linked with limitation of thought—tell us that there may be lying dormant in him a capacity for greater life, which may be exercised when he, a dead man, shall have risen from among the dead.

The only character whom I have neglected is the inspector of the baths, and I hasten to do him tardy, but scant, justice. He is neither more nor less than the average inspector of baths. But he is that.

So much for the characterization, which is at all times profound and interesting. But apart from the characters in the play, there are some noteworthy points in the frequent and extensive side-issues of the line of thought. The most salient of these is what seems, at first sight, nothing more than an accidental scenic feature. I allude to the environment of the drama. One cannot but observe in Ibsen's later work a tendency to get out of closed rooms. Since *Hedda Gabler* this tendency is most marked. The last act of *The Master Builder* and the last act of *John Gabriel Borkman* take place in the open air. But in this play the three acts are *al fresco*. To give heed to such details as these in the drama may be deemed ultra-Boswellian fanaticism. As a matter of fact it is what is barely due to the work of a great artist. And this feature, which is so prominent, does not seem to me altogether without its significance.

Again, there has not been lacking in the last few social dramas a fine pity for men— a note nowhere audible in the uncompromising rigour of the early eighties. Thus in

the conversion of Rubek's views as to the girl-figure in his masterpiece, "The Resurrection Day," there is involved an all-embracing philosophy, a deep sympathy with the cross-purposes and contradictions of life, as they may be reconcilable with a hopeful awakening—when the manifold travail of our poor humanity may have a glorious issue. As to the drama itself, it is doubtful if any good purpose can be served by attempting to criticize it. Many things would tend to prove this. Henrik Ibsen is one of the world's great men before whom criticism can make but feeble show. Appreciation, hearkening is the only true criticism. Further, that species of criticism which calls itself dramatic criticism is a needless adjunct to his plays. When the art of a dramatist is perfect the critic is superfluous. Life is not to be criticized, but to be faced and lived. Again, if any plays demand a stage they are the plays of Ibsen. Not merely is this so because his plays have so much in common with the plays of other men that they were not written to cumber the shelves of a library, but because they are so packed with thought. At some chance expression the mind is tortured with some question, and in a flash long reaches of life are opened up in vista, yet the vision is momentary unless we stay to ponder on it. It is just to prevent excessive pondering that Ibsen requires to be acted. Finally, it is foolish to expect that a problem, which has occupied Ibsen for nearly three years, will unroll smoothly before our eyes on a first or second reading. So it is better to leave the drama to plead for itself. But this at least is clear, that in this play Ibsen has given us nearly the very best of himself. The action is neither hindered by many complexities, as in *The Pillars of Society*, nor harrowing in its simplicity, as in *Ghosts*. We have whimsicality, bordering on extravagance, in the wild Ulfheim, and subtle humour in the sly contempt which Rubek and Maja entertain for each other. But Ibsen has striven to let the drama have perfectly free action. So he has not bestowed his wonted pains on the minor characters. In many of his plays these minor characters are matchless creations. Witness Jacob Engstrand, Tönnesen, and the demonic Molvik! But in this play the minor characters are not allowed to divert our attention.

On the whole, *When We Dead Awaken* may rank with the greatest of the author's work—if, indeed, it be not the greatest. It is described as the last of the series, which began with *A Doll's House*—a grand epilogue to its ten predecessors. Than these dramas, excellent alike in dramaturgic skill, characterization, and supreme interest, the long roll of drama, ancient or modern, has few things better to show.

E. M. Forster

Ibsen the Romantic

"My book is poetry, and if it is not poetry, then it will be."—IBSEN to BJÖRNSON

IBSEN was a poet during the earlier part of his life. He began as a lyricist, and his first plays are either in verse or are inspired by an imaginative contemplation of the past. When he was about forty, a change occurred, the importance of which has been differently estimated. Certain critics, both friendly and hostile, regard it as a fundamental change. They argue that with *The League of Youth* the real or realistic Ibsen begins to emerge, the singer dies, the social castigator is born, the scene clarifies and darkens, and ideas come to the front which do not necessarily contradict previous ideas, but which are given a prominence that entirely alters the dramatic emphasis. We pass from the epic to the domestic. Peer Gynt becomes Hialmar Ekdal, and Brand as Gregers Werle tears the spectacles of illusion from his eyes, and they work out their tragedy not among forests and fjords, but in a photographic studio opening into a sort of aviary. The aviary contains a few dead Christmas trees, also a water trough, some rabbits but no bears, one wild duck and that a damaged one. We could not be further from romance, the critics say, and turn, if we are friendly, to the character drawing, the technique, and the moral and social issues; if they are hostile, to the squalor. "Somewhere in the course of the battle of his life Ibsen had a lyric Pegasus killed under him," writes Brandes. "Novel and perilous nonsense," wrote the *Daily Telegraph*. The critics agree in thinking that the poetry, if ever there was any, has gone.

Has it gone? Can the habits of forty years be set aside? Of twenty years—yes; most people are romantic at twenty, owing to lack of experience. As they grow older life offers various alternatives, such as worldliness or philosophy or the sense of humour, and they usually accept one of these. If, in spite of more solid temptations, they still cling to poetry, it is because a deep preference has to be satisfied. Ibsen was a poet at forty because he had that preference. He was a poet at sixty also. His continued interest in avalanches, water, trees, fire, mines, high places, travelling, was not accidental. Not only was he born a poet—he died one, and as soon as we try to understand him instead of asking him to teach us, the point becomes clearer.

He is, of course, not easy to understand. Two obstacles may be noted. In the first place although he is not a teacher he has the air of being one, there is something in his method that implies a message, though the message really rested on passing irritabilities, and not on any permanent view of conduct or the universe. In the second place, he further throws us off the scent by taking a harsh or a depressing view of human relationships. As a rule, if a writer has a romantic temperament, he will find human relationships beautiful. His characters may hate one another or be unhappy together, but they will generate nobility or charm, they will never be squalid, whatever their other defects. And the crux in Ibsen is that, though he had the romantic temperament, he found personal intercourse sordid. Sooner or later his characters draw their little knives, they rip up the present and the past, and the closer their intimacy the better their opportunities for exchanging pain. Oswald Alving knows how to hurt his mother, Rosmer his mistress, and married couples are even more favourably placed. The Helmers, the Tesmans, the Wangels, Solnesses, Allmers, Borkmans, Rubeks— what a procession, equally incapable of comradeship and ecstasy! If they were heroic or happy once, it was before the curtain rose, and only survives as decay. And if they attain reconciliation, like the Rentheim sisters, the curtain has to fall. Their intercourse is worse than unfriendly, it is petty; moral ugliness trespasses into the æsthetic. And when a play is full of such characters and evolves round their fortunes, how can it possibly be a romantic play? Poetry might perhaps be achieved if Ibsen's indignation was of the straight-hitting sort, like Dante's. But for all its sincerity there is something automatic about it, he reminds us too often of father at the breakfast table after a bad night, sensitive to the defects of society as revealed by a chance glance at the newspaper, and apt to blame all parties for them indiscriminately. Now it is the position of women that upsets father, now the lies people tell, now their inability to lie, now the drains, now the newspaper itself, which he crumples up, but his helpers and servers have to retrieve it, for bad as are all political parties he must really see who got in at Rosmersholm. Seldom can a great genius have had so large a dose of domestic irritability. He was cross with his enemies and friends, with theatre-managers, professors, and students, and so cross with his countrymen for not volunteering to help the Danes in 1864 that he had to go to Italy to say so. He might have volunteered in person—he was in the prime of life at the time—but this did not occur to him, he preferred instead to write a scathing little satire about a Norwegian mother whose son was safe at the front. And it is (if one may adopt the phrase) precisely the volunteer spirit that is absent from his conception of human relationships. He put everything into them except the strength of his arm.

"Not a great writer . . . almost great, but marred by this lack of generosity." How readily the phrases rise to the lips! How false they are! For this nagging quality, this habitual bitterness—they are essential in his greatness, because they beckon to the poetry in him, and carry it with them under the ground. Underground. Into the depths of the sea, the depths of the sea. Had he been of heroic build and turned to the light and the sun, his gifts would have evaporated. But he was—thank heaven—subterranean, he loved narrow passages and darkness, and his later plays have a romantic intensity which not only rivals the romantic expansion of their predecessors, but is absolutely unique in literature. The trees in old Ekdal's aviary are as numerous as a forest because they are countless, the water in the chickens' trough includes all the waves on which the Vikings could sail. To his impassioned vision dead and damaged things, however contemptible socially, dwell for ever in the land of romance, and this is the secret of his so-called symbolism; a connection is found between objects that lead different types of existence; they reinforce one another and each lives more intensely than before. Consequently his stage throbs with a mysteriousness for which no obvious preparation has been made, with beckonings, tremblings, sudden compressions of the air, and his characters as they wrangle among the oval tables and stoves are watched by an unseen power which slips between their words.

A weaker dramatist who had this peculiar gift would try to get his effect by patches of fine writing, but with Ibsen as with Beethoven the beauty comes not from the tunes, but from the way they are used and are worked into the joints of the action. *The Master Builder* contains superb examples of this. The plot unfolds logically, the diction is flat and austere, the scene is a villa close to which another villa is being erected, the chief characters are an elderly couple and a young woman who is determined to get a thrill out of her visit, even if it entails breaking her host's neck. Hilda is a minx, and though her restlessness is not as vulgar as Hedda Gabler's it is quite as pernicious and lacks the saving gesture of suicide. That is one side of Hilda. But on the other side she touches Gerd and the Rat Wife and the Button Moulder, she is a lure and an assessor, she comes from the non-human and asks for her kingdom and for castles in the air that shall rest on solid masonry, and from the moment she knocks at the door poetry filters into the play. Solness, when he listened to her, was neither a dead man nor an old fool. No prose memorial can be raised to him, and consequently Ibsen himself can say nothing when he falls from the scaffolding, and Bernard Shaw does not know that there is anything to say. But Hilda hears harps and voices in the air, and though her own voice may be that of a sadistic schoolgirl the sound has nevertheless gone out into the dramatist's universe, the avalanches in *Brand* and *When We Dead Awaken* echo it, so does the metal in John Gabriel Borkman's mine. And it has all been done so competently. The symbolism never holds up the action, because it is part of the action, and because Ibsen was a poet, to whom creation and craftsmanship were one. It is the same with the white horse in *Rosmersholm*, the fire of life in *Ghosts*, the gnawing pains in *Little Eyolf*, the sea in *The Lady from the Sea*, where Hilda's own stepmother voices more openly than usual the malaise that connects the forces of nature and the fortunes of men. Everything rings true and echoes far because it is in the exact place which its surroundings require.

The source of Ibsen's poetry is indefinable; presumably it comes from the same place as his view of human nature, otherwise they would not harmonize as they do in his art. The vehicle in which poetry reached him—that can easily be defined; it was, of course, the scenery of western and south-western Norway. At some date previous to his Italian journey he must have had experiences of passionate intensity among the mountains, comparable to the early experiences of Wordsworth in the English lakes. All his life they kept returning to him, clothed in streams, trees, precipices, and hallowing his characters while they recriminated. In *Brand* and *Peer Gynt* they filled the stage; subsequently they shrank and concentrated; in the two last plays they again fill the stage and hasten the catastrophes by a shroud of snow. To compare Ibsen with Wordsworth is to scandalize the faithful in either camp, yet they had one important point in common: they were both of them haunted until the end of their lives by the romantic possibilities of scenery. Wordsworth fell into the residential fallacy; he continued to look at his gods direct, and to pin with decreasing success his precepts to the flanks of Helvellyn. Ibsen, wiser and greater, sank and smashed the Dovrëfjeld in the depths of the sea, the depths of the sea. He knew that he should find it again. Neither his satire nor his character drawing dwelt as deep; neither the problems he found in human conduct nor the tentative solutions he propounded lay at the roots of his extraordinary heart. There, in that strange gnarled region, a primaeval romanticism lurked, frozen or twisted or exuding slime, there was the nest of the great Boyg. The Great Boyg did not strive, did not die, lay beneath good and evil, did not say one thing more than another:

Forward or back, and it's just as far;
Out or in, and it's just as strait.

What do the words mean, and, apart from their meaning, are they meant to be right? And if right, are the prayers of Solveig, which silence them for a moment, wrong? It is proper that we should ask such questions as these when focussing on the moral and social aspect of his work, and they have been brilliantly asked and answered by Bernard Shaw. But as soon as we shift the focus the questions go dim, the reformer becomes a dramatist, we shift again and the dramatist becomes a lyric poet, listening from first to last for the movements of the trolls. Ibsen is at bottom Peer Gynt. Side whiskers and all, he is a boy bewitched:

> The boy has been sitting on his mother's lap.
> They two have been playing all the life-day
> long.

And though the brow that bends over him can scarcely be described as maternal, it will assuredly preserve him from the melting ladle as long as books are read or plays seen.

Daniel Haakonsen

Ibsen the Realist

IN THIS study, the intention is to investigate Ibsen's realism as it manifests itself in certain of those dramas of contemporary life that fill the later years of his authorship. Before attempting to define the problem, let us remind ourselves of some of the more concrete impressions we gain from an Ibsen performance. Let us, on a very elementary level, first attempt to note the realism in the action, the dialogue, and the conflict of character, so that we may have something substantial to work from.

To begin with, let us take three separate and unusual points of view: one for the action, one for the dialogue, and one for the conflict of character. What is unusual about each of them is simply that they are not particularly demanding. They are limited to a few simple impressions only. In the first place we adopt a point of view which will allow the *action*—in the outward sense —to define itself in as concrete and elementary a fashion as possible.

Imagine that we are present in the theatre during a performance of *A Doll's House*— but assume that we act as though we were deaf. We refrain from listening to the dialogue, and content ourselves with observing the movements of the central character on the stage. Such an assumed deafness during the performance of a French classical tragedy would mean only a long evening of boredom. It would be tiresome to watch men and women on the stage whose eyes were directed, as it were, upon another world and who spoke their litanies of verse which we had agreed not to listen to. Shakespeare's *Hamlet* would no doubt be better able to hold our interest by virtue of its external action and its setting, but we would probably be tempted beyond endurance to listen more than once when the audience around us was particularly deeply moved. For at those moments the hero would be standing motionless, with or without a skull in his hands, and delivering his lines—words fraught with deep significance, apparently.

Not that Nora herself is exactly dumb. But she entertains us splendidly by means of her overt movements alone. She enters with her arms full of parcels which she unloads on a table. The door behind her stands open, and outside we see a delivery man handing a Christmas tree over to the maid. Nora goes back to pay the man. She resists his move to give her change, shuts the door, and takes off her outdoor things in the room. Then she fishes a little paper bag out of her pocket, helps herself to one or two macaroons, and eats them as she holds the bag in her hand. She walks cautiously over to another of the doors and listens, and then she comes back again to the table with its parcels. All at once she stuffs the bag back into her pocket and wipes her mouth. The door opens and a man comes on the stage from that side room where Nora had stopped and listened. Thereupon a long conversation ensues.

But those of us who do not listen to the words are by no means bored—Nora keeps us alert. She opens parcels to show what she has bought for Christmas, all except one which she makes great play of keeping back. And during the rest of the conversa-

From *Henrik Ibsens realisme*, Aschehoug, Oslo, 1957, translated by the editor, and published by permission.

tion she adopts a series of lively and recognizable attitudes, seemingly as though to entertain. Now she is like a little schoolgirl being questioned, now she is clearly being scolded and chastised—in fun. She sulks for a moment, she then puts her hand over her husband's mouth, she toys with his coat buttons. Then she is a little girl again, clapping her hands for joy. During her interrogation at one point she walks away from her husband, but at other times she is so close that his arm comes round her. She radiates joy when she is given money, which she then proceeds to count. In a word, she is incessantly on the move.

Nora's movements take on the aspect almost of a secret dance, the opening steps of which are constantly being broken off and replaced by something else. Yet it is quite evident that there is unity and meaning in all her activity. What accounts for this duality?

The interrupted quality of her movements is due to encounters with things. We recognize on the stage a reality which does not belong exclusively to the theatre but belongs also to ordinary life. The room that takes shape round Nora's ballet is a real one, not some ideal place which is a rendezvous for the lovers at one moment, and serves for a public meeting the next. The setting is created as a framework round an everyday intermezzo, and consists of real objects that Nora must constantly be ready to acknowledge in her behaviour. The table stands in the middle because the parcels lie there, just as in a later scene it stands in the centre because Nora hides under the table while she is playing with her children. And there are a great many other *things*—doors, buttons, money, macaroons —that split up her interest and her movements. Moreover, if one looks round at Ibsen's other plays, one constantly sees the same thing happening. Concrete objects like cases, armchairs, books, papers, hats, photograph albums are always either inviting some movements towards them, or else repelling such approaches. They form the poles which the basic action must conform to, even if it means a constantly interrupted and altered choreography.

And what is then the *unifying* principle? What is it that orders things so that the result is not chaos? The answer is not one that leads us *beyond* Ibsen's realism. What serves to combine these various impressions in our minds is the recognition of an intermezzo from everyday life. A snapshot from ordinary living, a situation from an ordinary family home, is introduced onto the stage and subjects the movements there to its law. The opening scene of *A Doll's House* is based on the situation of a young wife returning home from Christmas shopping on the morning of Christmas Eve. The tree, the tipping, the husband's curiosity, the extra allowance—all these are constituents of this one situation, particularly when we add that the financial status of this household is about to change radically and that a weight is being lifted from the wife's mind. Hence the reason for the light-footed dance among the parcels, the doors, and the coat buttons. She has already begun to adapt her home to the new and more favourable economic conditions.

The *things* serve to fragment, but the situation consolidates; the direct and familiar realities of life play their part in both instances. And taking shape behind this situation is a completely new condition in the house, which is the first preliminary for the larger action; the expectant mind is directed towards some objective. This expected development may ultimately turn out to be something rather more than merely the economic improvement in the family, but for the moment the latter provides a basis. And wherever we direct our attention—towards the interrupted steps of the dance, towards the unified situation, or towards the new condition in the house that heralds the larger action—we meet a reality that is concrete and living. This first point of view which we have defined supports the assumption that Ibsen is a truly realistic writer.

Let us now try with a different and more limited point of view. This time let us gain some impression of the living nature of Ibsen's dialogue, by uncovering our ears as we witness once again the same scene we have just experienced as deaf spectators. We pay particular attention to the words and the intonation that best make us aware of the inner movement, the pulsating life in the conversation.

The first thing we come in contact with is a series of affective cries that reflect either a state of mind or a momentary experience:

Bought, did you say? All that? . . . Oh, but Torvald. . . . Oh, you know. . . . Puh! We can borrow in the meantime. . . . Oh, don't say such horrid things. . . . Nora, Nora! Just like a woman! . . . There, there. . . . Oh, thank you, thank you! . . . Oh, but Torvald. . . . No denying it, Nora my dear. . . . Yes it is, Nora, that sort of thing is inherited. . . . Now, now. . . . Oh, that's marvellous! . . . Oh, how absolutely marvellous to hear that! . . . Oh, there's the bell. . . . That's a pity. . . .

We also note that the characters speak out fairly often about the things that affect them. They explain to the other person, or they clarify for themselves, their own peculiarities or their own attitude towards a particular question. As an example from the scene we have just been considering, one might mention Nora's remark:

As a matter of fact I save everything I can.

And Helmer laughs as he replies:

Yes, you are right there. Everything you *can*. But you simply can't. . . . What a funny little one you are! Just like your father. Always on the lookout for money, wherever you can lay hands on it. But as soon as you've got it, it just seems to slip through your fingers.

In the following scene, the conversation between Nora and Mrs Linde, it is Nora herself who discourses about her own qualities and peculiarities:

Nora. . . . Oh, Kristine, I'm so happy and relieved. I must say it's lovely to have plenty of money and not have to worry. Isn't it?

Mrs Linde. Yes, it must be nice to have enough, at any rate.

Nora. No, not just enough, but pots and pots of money!

Mrs Linde (smiling). Nora, Nora, haven't you learned any sense yet? At school you used to be an awful spendthrift.

Nora. Yes, Torvald still says I am. (Wags her finger.) But little Nora isn't as stupid as everybody thinks. . . .

Naturally, most characters in drama have this tendency to reveal in conversation their inmost selves under emotional stress, or in more balanced moments to try to explain themselves and what they think and believe. But in Ibsen's social dramas the characteristic thing about such revelations is that they never fully complete themselves. Feeling comes through the dialogue, but one gets only a brief glimpse of it before it is gone and replaced by something new, which in its turn must give way a moment later. Something similar happens with the more direct manifestations of what the characters are thinking and feeling. They begin to take shape, to sketch a picture of the speaker or the person spoken about. But scarcely is one aware of this before the characterisation is interrupted in the same fashion as Nora's secret dance. One might contrast this with the great monologues in French classical tragedy. There, the hero is given an opportunity to clarify his entire situation, to communicate all the essence of his inner thoughts and emotions without interruption. Nobody is rushed. There is no sponge here that comes along and wipes out everything on the board to make room for what is new; rather the writing goes on to cover the walls and the ceiling.

So again the question arises: what accounts for the peculiar quality of form in Ibsen, in this instance, in his dialogue?

The fragmentation derives from the fact that in their conversation the characters react to *real* topics and problems. The thoughts and emotions and inner life of the characters manifest themselves in connection with some everyday problem (shopping, borrowing, etc.) but then, so to speak, they momentarily encounter the other person's reaction to the same thing, or else the feeling that the topic is too dangerous to allow of anything more about it being said to the other person. Conversation is a long chain of collisions between temperaments, because the people who are placed in relationship to each other are both immersed in a world of actual things, and they interpret (fleetingly) their own inner life by the help of these things.

In everyday life outside the theatre, we are accustomed to rapid and as it were restless changes in the topic of conversation, and to the fact that our inner thoughts and feelings express themselves briefly as the occasion presents itself and then passes again. The mind is not necessarily disturbed so long as the conversational changes follow the usual social rules. In respect of conversation, there is a set of handy conventions or patterns: people talk about *this* but not about *that*; this is what one says to the hostess on arrival, and this on departure; changes of topic must be in accordance with a certain degree of logic, but more than that sounds pedantic. . . . And it then becomes clear that precisely here lies the unifying principle of Ibsen's dialogue. The dramatist has applied this pattern to the stage, and with a sure touch has so ordered the speeches that we immediately recognize ourselves in it, and feel at home.

It is quite true that, objectively speaking, the opening dialogue in *A Doll's House* throws us back and forth between a series of little topics and little outbursts of feeling. But, looked at from the point of view of real life, the conversation is ordered—ordered to a greater degree than the real-life conversations which the patterns and conventions are made for. When the wife has been to town to buy presents, and the husband has torn himself away from his study to view the collection, what is more probable than that the conversation should begin with the household expenses? Helmer

reacts in the first instance as many husbands, both then and now, would by talking about the money that has been "squandered." And if, as in the play, the husband has only recently taken a better-paid job, it is quite natural that one of the parties should refer to the better economic prospects in view. This in its turn provokes a brief exchange on the business of taking a loan, and only after the husband has expressed himself on this topic does the attention turn to the parcels which the wife displays and comments on, to show how clever her purchases have been.

It is probably this pattern, approximating as it does so closely to real life, and serving to unite what the quick reciprocal reactions have fragmented, that gives Ibsen's dialogue its *conversational* stamp. Conversation is not, as one might be tempted to suppose, something commonplace in the theatre; on the contrary it is one of the characteristic features of Ibsen's drama. One would hardly say that Hamlet converses with his father's ghost, or that Racine's Phèdre converses with her stepson Hippolyte about the passion she feels for him and cannot subdue. But in Ibsen's plays there is, so to speak, no dialogue that is not adapted in some form or other to conversation.

Take, for example, the first meeting between Pastor Manders and Regine in *Ghosts*. There is so much in their dialogue, it is so shot through with secret passion, that a Racine would have been able to create great pathos from the material in it. But Ibsen has chosen to build his dialogue to the most natural conversational pattern imaginable, if not to say the most banal. A few words introduce it, first about the steamer that presumably must already have arrived, seeing that the Pastor is already in the doorway, and then about the rain that has made his journey rather an uncomfortable one. The Pastor, very naturally, asks how things are in the house, and remarks that Regine has grown since he last saw her. So much for the introduction. Manders and

Regine have a common problem—Regine's father—and the conversation turns to him. And then finally Regine can turn to what most concerns her, and what the visitor might be expected to interest himself in— she wants to return to town and earn some money. The conversation ends with the Pastor asking Regine to fetch her mistress. A little abrupt, perhaps, but nevertheless within the framework of a tone acceptable between caller and servant. If Manders had had to break that tone, he would possibly have been a greater threat than he is as things are. But the form is maintained, and the mind is quickly at rest. Such a conversation might have stood as a kind of model in a book on *Tact and Good Taste,* in a chapter on "the arriving guest." Yet it was by no means inevitable that the things that occupied the minds of these two characters should have been able to find expression within a *conversational* framework at all.

Thus, in Ibsen's dialogue we first make contact with the nervous and fragmented life of the emotions, and secondly with the *conversation* that resolves the many bristling reactions within a social order and context. And behind the conversation we suspect that the relationship between the characters, on a less elementary level, is a conflict within the framework of a far-reaching pattern of social behaviour. The atmosphere is charged with strong opposition, but the ties that unite are also correspondingly strong. But no matter whether we attend to the little reactions to concrete things, or to the conversation, or to the social structures which we sense behind and beyond, in each case we are always in contact with real life.

Let us therefore finally take a third restricted view of the material—this time to get at the real nature of the conflict between characters in Ibsen's plays. Let us follow a character through the opening moments of one act to see how he comes in conflict with himself—still on a completely elementary and concrete level.

Hjalmar Ekdal in *The Wild Duck* is, in Act I, at a dinner party at Mr Werle's. In this house there is good food and good drink, and Hjalmar would enjoy himself very well—or, at any rate, adequately—if only he could be left in peace. He therefore attaches a great deal of importance to *being* in peace; his whole character seems to be directed to this aim. But the son of the house whispers in his ear that he must take part in the conversation—it is all part and parcel of things. And Hjalmar resolves this little conflict by submitting to pressure: he joins in the conversation and at once draws attention to his own ignorance. Thereafter all he wants is to be left in peace again, and just talk to his childhood friend about his own quiet good fortune and his own quiet melancholy. But then the door opens, and his own father, uninvited and unexpected, toddles through the room; and it is made clear that his family do not belong here. Hjalmar turns aside to avoid another unpleasantnesses. But a near-sighted guest asks him—*him!*—who it was who came through. Hjalmar is again in conflict and tries to twist away—he says he did not see. But then his friend comes and calls him to account: You stand there and deny your own father? It is almost incredible how much can interfere with a man's quiet, unpretentious existence. Hjalmar decides to go home, but forgets to take back with him a little treat for his daughter, as he had promised. So he is deprived of peace in his own home, too, because of those things he is expected to do. The things a father has to remember. . . .

We need not pursue him any further in this, but no doubt the torments and the innumerable little conflicts can be relied on to do it for us: the wife who comes out with her malapropisms while educated people are present, the people who turn up demanding to be photographed when the photographer wants time off, the daughter's eyes that have to be considered if any retouching work is left for her to do. Hjalmar Ekdal may not exactly be "assailed by an army of sorrows," as he himself puts it, but he is tormented by life. However much he twists and turns in his search for a happy and untroubled life, conflicts meet him on all sides.

But behind the many small conflicts that can torment even a person outside the theatre—especially if he is sensitive and wants nothing more than to be left in peace —behind these there is a more boldly defined conflict with reality to be considered. The objectives of the main Ibsen characters are many and various, from wealth, power, and honour on all kinds of sublime or trivial levels, to love and the development of creative talents. But whatever this goal or ideal may be, there is generally a kind of spaciousness attached to it: a spaciousness in behaviour or in income or in circumstance, or a spaciousness in moral outlook or in action that means freedom and, in favourable circumstances, human dignity. This need for spaciousness is to be taken together with the fact that life puts its trivialities in the way of Ibsen's characters. On a more comprehensive level than the one on which we chose to observe Hjalmar Ekdal—but still in close contact with the smaller irritations—we see Ibsen's characters having to face gossip and rumour, moral bigotry and narrow-mindedness, economic worries and the letter of the law —in short all the demands and ties that bind a person's existence and threaten to put his freedom in chains.

The conflicts of character that arise on this basis are of an entirely different significance from those we find in *Oedipus Rex, Macbeth,* or *Polyeucte.* They are moreover "realistic" in the meaning the word has in literary history, for it is precisely this tension between the yearning of the human soul and the circumstances of everyday life that is the basis of the kind of psychology the realists were concerned with. It received perhaps its most characteristic expression in Flaubert's novel *Madame Bovary,* but it can be found everywhere in the literature of realism.

In Ibsen's case, one might say that this tension sucks up into itself the whole chaotic multiplicity of small conflicts—and at the same time gives us a glimpse at a deeper level of some dependence on other laws. Ibsen's characters do not find it easy to escape the demands that are made on them from without. They have certain feelings of guilt, arising either from some real transgression or simply from the *wish* to break with the usual standards, which in their own eyes involves them in guilt. They feel a burden of duty even in respect of the moral order that determines that duty; they feel their hearts only half in sympathy with it, and sometimes not even that. But such feelings of guilt are entirely rational in so far as society demonstrably has the power to create them—or resolve them—in the individual.

All three points of view which we have considered support the idea that Ibsen's realism is something belonging to the essence of his drama. One might add finally that the author's fidelity to external reality is such that it is comparatively easy to indicate the actual form of existence that served him as a model. He steadily explored a well-defined social institution as it existed in nineteenth-century Norway, and has given it a deathless monument: I am thinking of the bourgeois [*bürgerlich*] family. All the twelve dramas of contemporary life between *Pillars of Society* and *When We Dead Awaken* are linked in the matter of milieu to it.

The bourgeois family is of course in itself an honourable institution. In its present form it goes back in a fairly direct line to the Middle Ages, but its roots go back further still. It embraces traditions which, although perhaps not comparable with that of the country [*bonde*] family, are no less worthy of respect. It has had many variants, but at different times and in different ways it has always organised its life around its temple—the house. Social and occupational stratification has also made for certain big differences.

The kind of bourgeois family favoured

by Ibsen has certain clearly defined characteristics. Its centre of gravity lies somewhere among the liberal academic professions, with a certain margin on each side: on the one hand it is open to the landed estates in the country and the attendant professional positions, and on the other hand it is open to the urban occupations with a certain artistic element: photographers, master builders, perhaps the occasional businessman with some eye for things beyond his work.

From a historical point of view, Ibsen's family owes something to the bourgeois "salon" culture that reached its peak in the eighteenth century, but was also very active both in the preceding century and in the succeeding one. This may seem paradoxical, for the author's native country was one of the places in Europe where this bourgeois "salon" life—like the age of chivalry earlier—was poorest, and where it left fewest traces. But it is nevertheless clear that this kind of "salon" life among the cultured middle classes, preferably as it flourished in a comparatively small place and among a few select people, is Ibsen's real domain. He is unrivalled in his ability to capture the essence of indoor conversation between people of that class of society that for many centuries has made a speciality of *domestic* living. It is not so much a matter of getting the "salon" tone proper among *company*—such as one finds in Molière's *Misanthrope* —but rather of revealing the atmosphere and the "homely" tone of life as lived among the family itself and its regular friends and its occasional guest—a tone somewhere between the elegance of the salon and the banalities of everyday talk.

Alongside the occupational characteristics and the rather French quality from the salon, one can also detect an English trait in the family Ibsen describes: the Victorian element is unmistakable. Certain topics are not talked about in polite society. The chance of any piquant conversation is comparatively small, the danger of scandal great. And the demand for respectability

and for conformity to the morals of society is so strong that it plays a considerable part in the conflict between one's wishes and one's obligations. In spite of all their individualistic qualities, the people who populate Ibsen's dramas are expressly social beings.

Fifty years ago, all the above indications of realism in Ibsen's modern plays would have tended—in the eyes not only of the public but also of the critics and literary historians—to be regarded as merits, if not indeed as triumphs. But realism today no longer enjoys the same high regard. Many reputable critics have been concerned to revise the conception that then prevailed about the nature and purpose of literature, and the revisions often apply also to the value attaching to the literary products of the age of realism. Some critics are content with a rather more relative revision: realism is allotted its place as one of a whole series of literary doctrines that have been advanced in more recent times, and a carefully balanced attitude is taken towards its products. Others feel constrained to allude to it as a misguided doctrine, believing that its view of art and literature is clearly inadequate.

It might seem, under these circumstances, that one would have to predict some diminution in people's estimate of and interest in Ibsen's works—at least for a time. One can no longer declare that Ibsen is a realist without delivering his works to a form of criticism that is considerably better equipped to see the limitations of realism than, for example, the adherents of the expressionist theatre were in the Twenties. The prestige of realism is threatened—but is it therefore necessarily lost?

Before attempting to answer, let us define one simple point. It is easier for us today than it was for the people of the 1870's and 1880's to see that the close attachment to everyday life that one finds in Ibsen's dramas has been quite consciously avoided by many other writers because they thought it constituted a danger to dramatic art. It was precisely for the reason that they did not want a tragic character to be seen fingering a jacket button, or eavesdropping outside a study door. Sophocles' Antigone is not to have parcels under her arm and coats to take off when she comes on the stage. If Racine's Phèdre ever had a sweet tooth, we at least never get any glimpse of that side of her nature. If housekeeping expenses in one form or another ever had any reality for the Macbeths, they at least avoid going into them while they are on stage. And if it might ever be thought that Corneille's Pauline could hide herself under the table while playing with her children, it is presumably the last position Corneille would choose to show her in. The everyday tone and the fragmented confidences that Ibsen excels in are just the things that certain dramatists would shun like the plague. Why not rather insert a monologue where necessary, so that the hero has a chance to interpret his emotional life on a level proper to it?

At the same time it is easier for us today to see that the view of dramatic art touched on above is by no means the result of ineptitude, as many were tempted to suppose by the rather naïve conception of realism that at one time prevailed—earlier dramatists could not of course know everything of Ibsen's pioneering methods, it was admitted, but if only they had . . . ! In other words, strong traditions in European drama and literature are opposed to Ibsen —less because the thought of literary realism was impossible in early ages than because earlier writers preferred other methods. The audience was not to be invited to forget that it was sitting in a theatre. It is not by reason of the illusion created but rather by the very lack of illusion that a play elevates and liberates itself and reaches the intensity such dramatists aspire to. In much great drama, the distance from everyday life is one of the central assumptions the play rests on.

Most people would probably agree thus far today. It is no doubt less obvious that the truly "realistic problem" is still untouched by the considerations we have just mentioned. It is in itself no telling objection to Ibsen to indicate that other writers preferred to write differently. His realism becomes a dubious thing only if it can be shown that external reality, in addition to giving him his material, also provides him with the ultimate norm and principles for the treatment of it; or, more precisely, only if the close attachment he has to everyday reality has a decisive influence over the creative process itself, over the means he uses to stylize his material and adapt it to the genuine demands of literature and the theatre.

If we strip realism of any doctrinaire aura and say that it denotes a method of treating the material that is close to reality, then it is clear that most great dramatists have at one time or another been realists. Shakespeare allows himself at times a dialogue so realistic that Ibsen would have blushed to follow him. If Ibsen's attachment to an external social reality means only that he attempted, more systematically than most, to catch some of life's own freshness in his plot and dialogue, then his form of drama would present no very deep problem. In that case Ibsen would have said to each and every one of his great predecessors: "You are absolutely right; art demands some kind of liberation from reality, some metamorphosis of reality even, which one then incorporates into one's drama. But a great poet creates a metamorphosis no matter whether he chooses to present the death of Caesar in verse, or to give in prose a chat with a neighbour over the garden fence. Don't be misled by the first theorists of realism. Nobody believes any longer that everyday life will seem like life on the stage. A tape-recording of the family's noise over the dinner table or the buzz of the mothers' meeting over the teacups would fall completely flat and only be of interest to phoneticians. But I am a realist in a more timeless sense. I drew my material from everyday life just as you drew yours from history and legend, without letting myself be caught up by the material any more than you did. I think I may say that my hold over my art is just as authentic as your hold over yours. I have stylized my material just as you have yours—but I have taken care to cover up the joints in my composition. I am just as much an artist as you are, but it is part of my style that I pretend I am not."

Thus might Ibsen have spoken if his realism had avoided all the hazards and kept clear of the theories that many important critics of his age proclaimed. But it must be admitted that appearances are against him. We have seen how he saves the action and the dialogue—taking them on their elementary level—from complete dissolution. But we have also seen that the means he uses are the imitation of everyday situations and the employment of the pattern of everyday conversation for the stage. This *does* give a certain grip on art, but it lacks any real power. And now the fundamental features of his psychology.

In the age of romanticism, the conflicts between the individual and society still had the power to move deeply, for the romantics were in a position to acknowledge all aspects of their own individualism, sick and healthy alike, and allow them to do battle against a recognized opponent. But when the realistic writers of the 1860's, 1870's, and 1880's inherited these same conflicts, they were already rather threadbare—or, should one say, diluted by a less rigorous set of problems. It is all very well for Ibsen to concentrate the inner conflicts and feelings of guilt and urges to freedom; but when he burdens this basic situation with a specifically realistic social psychology, it admittedly remains an artistic expedient, but an expedient of dubiously small format. Human passion has then to be transposed down to a refined level, if the opposition it meets from outside consists in the most trivial obstacles the author can find.

In other words, the question is whether

Ibsen has allowed external reality to determine even the sweep of his creative activity, and whether much of the life in his plays is an illusion. Perhaps we accept his interiors, his dialogue, and his types because we are still familiar with the milieu they were taken from. We can still glimpse the models in the background. But as the nineteenth century's middle class and its attitudes and habits become more and more distant from us, may it not happen that larger and larger parts of Ibsen's works will fall into oblivion? Are not his characters too tied to a particular cultural epoch to be able to live on by their own strength?

Let us sum up the kind of criticism Ibsen seems to be exposed to in some words André Gide used earlier in this century in connection with the crisis in the theatre at that time. When a powerful creator of character like Ibsen (said Gide) "places habits and conventions about his characters' shoulders like some tiresome cloak, he at once condemns even the most heroic of them to defeat." And the meaning is clear: to defeat before the battle has really begun, to defeat without any genuine dramatic conflict. Gide was hoping for some Pygmalion or Prometheus of the theatre who would open up anew the gulf between the living room and the stage, between reality and poem, who would put the author at a distance from the audience and remove the cloak of social habit from the shoulders of the hero.

Thus we see that one of the most considerable literary critics of this century—a man moreover who has the greatest admiration for Ibsen's talents—hopes that a new poet will arise who can undo what Ibsen has done to the theatre. And the cause is clear enough. For Gide it is not simply that in external things Ibsen's characters belong to everyday life, and are transient. Habit, social custom, and conventional behaviour, all of which belong to the nature of realism, are in Ibsen's case wholly at one with their character. This "tiresome cape" Gide talks about—is it not precisely what we have been examining above: the patterns of behaviour and conversation and psychology which serve to stylize the lives of the characters on the stage, but which do not seem to offer them any opportunity of freely unfolding themselves, of revealing who they really are? And has not Ibsen put, in place of free creativity, merely verisimilitude and outward illusion? Has he not, like some dutiful servant of the society he rebels against, reproduced all the forms of social intercourse, and all the servitude they impose upon the heart and the mind?

Criticism directed against realism can thus assume dangerous proportions, and it clearly seems to have direct relevance to Ibsen. Must we then deliver his works defenceless into the hands of the anti-realist critics? What we can do to determine how far this kind of criticism can be sustained against Ibsen's works is to carry our gaze beyond the overt behaviour and the immediate situation, which have so far occupied our attention, and see how the pattern of everyday things takes shape on a rather more profound level. If Ibsen's characters are completely tied to their lives of middle-class respectability, this will also be evident in what happens to them on the stage and in the general context of their lives. A more comprehensive view of the composition must be able to show whether the characters live another life on a deeper level than the merely social, or whether the "cloak of society" condemns them to defeat. And we ask ourselves: What does the picture look like if we adopt this more extensive point of view?

It cannot be denied that, even by these wider perspectives, Ibsen's characters conduct themselves as social beings. Society plays a conspicuous role, either a friendly or a hostile one—in the present context it does not matter which. Ibsen's realistic heroes and heroines are directly concerned to behave *comme il faut*, for they have nearly always a position to maintain as the gentleman—or the lady—of a bourgeois household. The enemy can then appear from without, like Krogstad in *A Doll's House*, but his weapons are the moral rules and prejudices prevailing in society. By reason of the position that has to be defended, it is in fact in large measure these moral rules and prejudices that serve as the yardstick.

But these are nevertheless only temporary truths. On a deeper level, the action possesses a different, a deeper, and a freer ideal, or tends step by step to approach it. The main character has a "kingly thought" (as it is called in *The Pretenders*) on the level of human fellowship. Sometimes it is concentrated in some phrase like "the miraculous," or "the true marriage"; sometimes the state of affairs it envisages is a kind of reflection of the free Parisian life of the artist, or of life together between "free, happy, and noble people." But always it is directed towards a state of affairs where the only things that count are one's relationship to another person and one's relationship to one's own calling, without their coming into any inner conflict: it relates to a kind of perfect state where the will to sacrifice oneself for the sake of some partnership and the desire for the unhindered development of one's own personality are resolved into a higher unity.

A clear-cut and heightened objective of this kind lies beyond the ordinary bourgeois rules of life, and it creates a spaciousness, primarily in respect of morals. It comes as no surprise when we notice in how many instances an Ibsen character originally found his way *en route* to this goal as a result of some decision that disregarded society's moral and even legal injunctions. There is some point in the character's past—the point of departure for the purposeful life he is living in the present—that has to be kept concealed if he is not to be compromised. He has to preserve some secret if he is to have any secure basis for his ambitions in his present milieu—ambitions which of course go far beyond the cultural level of his surroundings. He is thus compelled to dissemble.

Nora Helmer behaves *comme il faut* as a wife in her own milieu, both when she respects Helmer's sense of dignity as a lawyer and as the family's breadwinner, and when she submits to his requests that she keep off sweets for the sake of her teeth. But her actions outside her husband's study door, with a bag of macaroons in her hand and then later in her pocket, show that she regards this form of dutifulness as a role she has been cast to play, and there is something similar about her attitude to money and to the law: she simply does not feel bound by her husband's views on these things. She has committed forgery in order to get hold of money that will take them abroad on a trip that will save his life. But she takes care that he does not find out. And this marks a situation that is characteristic both of her actions as a whole and of the actions of many other of Ibsen's characters: some form of dissimulation helps them to keep the past a secret and to hide their real attitude to things in the present.

But they are not, as one might hastily assume, thus free of the press of society. It becomes apparent that the dissimulation has a deeper effect than they had reckoned with. The occasion when they set their course across society's moral and judicial laws also brought them into opposition with their own aspirations, and in two respects. In the first place: the secret decision that one once made was also a decision made on behalf of a second person, somebody who both then and now has had to be kept out of it by the same pretence that one keeps up all round. When an accounting is finally called for—and inevitably there is always a final accounting—one finds oneself in conflict with the partnership that was a chief element in the ideal state one was striving for. And in the second place: this dissimulation for the sake of one's objective has prevented any proper realisation of one's personality, both in respect of society and of the second person involved—with the result that there is a betrayal even of one's own self-develop-

ment. One has involved oneself in serious guilt even in the light of one's own moral ambitions, so that an even deeper dread than the mere loss of society's outward respect lies at the root of things when the characters jealously preserve the secrets of the past, and themselves draw back from any too penetrating recognition of them.

Moreover, it was society that brought about the misfortune, and the question of guilt is considerably diluted by reason of the intimate and at the same time impersonal relationship that prevails with that society. Nora was so ignorant of the law when she committed her forgery that she even believed the law would applaud her actions. And it is like this almost everywhere in Ibsen's dramas: there is a curious mixture of ignorance, chance event, the compulsion of the moment, diminished consciousness and the like, which explains why one has somehow combined moral aspirations with some transgression, and thus delivered oneself into society's hands. In a deeper sense one is not guilty in what one has done; and any fully personal accounting with the past, or any personal relationship to the forces that have led one astray, seems to be excluded from the very first. But then where does it all lead—this relative emancipation from society as a result of some crime, this dissimulation, and this idealism so uncharacteristic of the middle classes? One is in any case defeated by powers that are too impersonal for one to come into real personal contact with.

In his analysis of *Ghosts*, Francis Fergusson has demonstrated perhaps more convincingly than anyone else the grand dramatic design that informs a characteristic Ibsen play. But when it comes to the composition of the piece as a whole, he can only reduce it to the level of a thriller: in the last resort, the main character has not found an adequate counterpart to enable her to meet her fate on the level it merits. And Fergusson is disposed to place Ibsen in a chapter that discusses the limitations of modern realism. For all his quite unusual ability to live himself into Ibsen's drama, his estimate is in line with Gide's.

It seems nevertheless as though the dramatist sits with a trump card in his hand. The state of affairs by which he seems to allow a series of chance events to exempt the characters from guilt, so that they can never raise themselves by some personal settlement above society—it is precisely this that proves on closer scrutiny to be a declaration that social determinism has been overcome, and that genuine human dimensions are preserved in the midst of Ibsen's realism.

How is this?

In the construction of his plays Ibsen attaches great importance to the revelation of what was hidden in the past. This revelation does not take place all at once. Ibsen makes use of what has been called a "retrospective technique": that is, he spreads the exposition out over the whole play. Little by little he lifts the veil on the ominous events of the past, in spite of the resistance the main character makes to this. To begin with there are only certain vague allusions: a tone of voice, a nuance of phrase, or an ambiguous remark, which allows it to be known that something once happened which it would be interesting to know about. As the play develops, we gradually get a better insight into the secret, until at a given point everything seems to stand clearly revealed; moreover there does not seem to be any talk of guilt on the part of the main character. Outward circumstance, with which he has no direct relationship, deprives him very largely of any personal responsibility.

But the fact that it seems so is nevertheless the result of the dramatist's cleverness. By making the whole play a continuous and continuing exposition, he accustoms us to expect more and more of the hidden past. One becomes in oneself more and more receptive to the secret side of things, more open to deeper implications. Admittedly the more precise revelations must inevitably come to a stop, but that does not mean that all communication ceases between a dramatist who has shown how profitable it is to search about in the past, and a spectator or reader who has accustomed himself to interpreting hints. It is exactly at this point that the most interesting things are communicated. The deepest secrets are not to be found in the past situation which the main character takes so much trouble to conceal, and the poet to reveal; nor in the outward explanations of how that situation ever came about. They are to be found rather in certain things that really do explain yet which are really kept concealed, perhaps the more firmly concealed the more explanatory they are. Ibsen's "retrospective technique" does not create its richest effects by the secrets it reveals, but by what it takes care not to reveal and merely lets us suspect—once we are in sympathy with that trend towards ever deeper-lying explanations which it sets moving, and which does not permit a stop to be made at any arbitrary time or any particular point.

The subjective innocence which one comes to attach to the past now shows itself in this larger context as something that prepares for the recognition that here is a guilt that goes deeper than ordinary guilt—that here is something related to the very essence of the character, something which relates to his personality and the very nature of his being. And in the same way the freedom aimed at becomes something very different from mere freedom from outward restraint, and becomes related to the entire spiritual existence of the individual. With this, social determinism is smashed like a shell. What this guilt and this profounder hope consist in varies from play to play. . . . But some things are common, at least in the family dramas after *A Doll's House* (this play being a transitional form), and they create an easily recognizable Ibsenist form of experiencing human fate: bathed in realism, but without the limitations of literary realism.

What is common to them is simple enough. It becomes clear that when one of

Ibsen's characters in the event is to sacrifice himself (or herself) on behalf of some partnership, he feels—but takes care not to formulate it too clearly to himself—that he had earlier delivered himself up to alien forces and is in an extremely weak and exposed position. And when in the event he freely wishes to assert his own personality, it becomes clear that he is willing to sacrifice the lives and existences of others to it. Ibsen's characters are directed towards a goal that demands consciousness of some obligation or some inferiority in their own person—and by a superiority so radical that it demands that all scruples must be set to one side.

Now it is not possible for Ibsen's characters to remove these claims from their own person—all they can do is to evade consciousness of them, at least for a time. This they do by a re-orientation in respect of their ideal objective, when this objective demands to be realized and when consciousness begins to obtrude: the objective becomes idealized in the sense that it elevates itself *above* reality, into the realm of daydream, illusion, or "pure" intellectual endeavour. And only when this ideal world has become a mixture of what was originally genuine idealism and some form or other of escapism can Ibsen's characters put their faith in it, shut themselves up in it as a defence against external demands—but with the consequence that sooner or later they have to face these demands and come to terms with more than that social life to which they tried to limit their awareness.

On such premises, Ibsen has in spite of all created a great dramatic form, a kind of tragedy of fate adapted to our own time, with perspectives that lead to the future. The tragedy of middle-class life [*bürgerliches Trauerspiel*], in the form he gave it, is populated by people who try to turn away from certain dimensions of spiritual life—dimensions which came as a supplement to the morals that defend social order and assure freedom in a limited field. An element of tragic irony about their ignorance causes guilt to build up, until finally there must come some crisis that speaks to the basic values of human existence. Finally the individual is brought face to face with fate itself.

It is difficult to imagine that the forces which poets of earlier ages selected as the forces of destiny should have been entirely wiped out. But in this age of science they keep themselves so well concealed that one easily remains in ignorance of their existence; and then, in spite of all mere chance explanations, it becomes a puzzle why a person his whole life long is hindered and frustrated in his development as a free person. That an individual fails to become what he would like to become and seems to have every opportunity of becoming is an eternal theme and a timeless experience, even though there are not so many in this age who see this, or who want to see it. Ibsen is one of those writers who have lifted the veil, to give some impression of what goes on under the surface, in the depths where man meets his fate, and where the big decisive things in life take place. And if one were to try to abstract the diagnosis his dramas implicitly make, it would surely be that man is paralyzed by his own greatness, and is too afraid of the evil and dangerous forces in his nature to be able to develop the good. Both the sense of obligation and the bold objectives that attach themselves to his being create a feeling of fear—fear of society, of one's fellows, but also presumably of greater powers. Ibsen often stimulates one to reflect that the fear of being dependent and unfulfilled and the fear of *hubris* and of self-aggrandisement are actually two sides of the same coin—a fear of the gods that is by no means Godfearing in a Christian sense, nor does it belong to any remote mythological stage in human development. Nor is it likely it ever will.

Hugo von Hofmannsthal

The People in Ibsen's Dramas

NOBODY, surely, has ever been tempted to entitle a lecture: "The People in Shakespeare's Plays"—or Otto Ludwig's or Goethe's—any more than entitling one "People in Real Life." Such a title would be pointless; after all, there is nothing there *except* people, three-dimensional, flesh-and-blood people who live out their lives, actively and passively; and everything lies in the fact of their existence. Apart from this, nothing else is intended or presumed. With Ibsen, the entire discussion, the enthusiasms and the repudiations, have nearly always been linked with something extraneous to the characters—with ideas, problems, prospects, reflections, moods.

Nevertheless there are also people in these plays; or rather, if one examines more closely, one person, a variant of a very rich, very modern, and very precisely observed human type. In addition there are background figures, dabs of contrasting colour; there are interpretive figures who criticize the main type and add details; and there are parallel figures, into whom certain individual traits of the main character are projected, which to some extent present a vividly illuminated aspect of the complete personality.

Despite the vast differences in other respects between the two individuals, it is precisely the same phenomenon that one finds in Byron; in both, there is this one constant figure with the mind of the author, with certain unfailing inner experiences, sometimes a little stylized, sometimes a little varied, but essentially one. In the one, it was called Manfred, Laura, Mazeppa, Tasso, Foscari, Childe Harold, the Giaour, the Corsair; it had a rather theatrical cloak, distorted features, a tremendous will, and the rhetoric of passionate and melancholy people; it was in essence a very straightforward and simple being. In the other, it is called Julian the Apostate, Hjalmar Ekdal, Peer Gynt, Lyngstrand, Dr. Helmer, Dr. Brendel, Dr. Rank; or Hedda, Ellida, Nora. It is by no means a simple being—indeed, it is very complicated; it speaks a nervous, clipped prose, without pathos and not always wholly intelligible; it takes itself ironically, it reflects about itself and copies itself. It is a continually varying product of its moods and of its own criticism of these moods.

All these people live a shadowy life; deeds and things play little part in their lives, which are made up almost exclusively of thoughts, moods, and moodiness. They want little; they do almost nothing. They think about thinking, feel themselves feeling, and practise auto-psychology. They delight in talking about themselves—although indeed they are often very unhappy—because to speak and to reflect is their real vocation. They are often writers: the Emperor Julian wears the robe of the philosopher and writes short, pretentious, and pedantic pamphlets; Hjalmar Ekdal and Ulrik Brendel will probably soon be publishing some epoch-making work, and Ejlert Lövborg has in fact already written one. Or they are languorous, sensitive, and artistic women, like the Lady from the Sea, and the other one who died in beauty. They lack all naïveté, they hold their life in their

From *Gesammelte Werke*, copyright 1950 by S. Fischer Verlag, Frankfurt am Main; Prosa I: "Die Menschen in Ibsens Dramen"; first published in 1893. Translated by Carla Hvistendahl and the editor. Published by permission.

hands, they finger it anxiously and want to give it meaning and style; they would like to submerge themselves in life, they would like something to come and carry them forcefully away and make them forget themselves. In them lives all the yearning of a Niels Lyhne: "Life, a poem! But not, however, in the sense that one always went about making poetry of one's life instead of living it. How meaningless that was, empty, empty, empty: this pursuit of oneself, cunningly observing one's own trail . . . this hurling oneself into the stream of life for the mere fun of it, then immediately fishing oneself out again and sitting there in some curious disguise! If only something would seize one—life, love, passion—so that one no longer wrote poetry, but instead oneself became the stuff of poetry."

This mysterious element, which is to come and carry one away and give life some great meaning, gives all things new colour and every word a soul—this thing has several names for these people. Sometimes it is the "miraculous" for which Nora longs; for Julian and Hedda it is Grecian, the great Bacchanalia, with noble grace and vine-leaves in one's hair; or it is the sea with its mysterious allure; or it is a free life on a grand pattern, in America or Paris. All these things are only symbolical names for something "out there," something "different." It is nothing other than Stendhal's yearning search for the "imprévu," for what is unforeseen, for what is not "weary, stale, flat, and unprofitable" in love and life. It is nothing but the dreamlonging of the romantics for the moonlit magic wilderness, for openings in the mountainside, for speaking pictures, for some undreamed-of fairy-tale element in life.

They live a narrow life, in unbearable, painful, depressing, yellow-grey, mean circumstances, and they all long to be away. Whenever someone promises to take them far away, they cry out, "Now at last I shall really live." They long to be away, as in grey and monotonous and unceasing rain

one longs for sunshine. "It seems to me," says one or the other of them, "that we do not live so very unlike fish in a pond. They have the fiord so close by, where the great, wild shoals of fish pass in and out. But the poor, tame, domestic fish know nothing of this; they are never allowed to join in." Some new revelation must come, they say, or a revelation of something new.

There is in this way of life a great deal of gossip and of irritating pettiness and monotony. In *Emperor and Galilean* there is court intrigue and academic intrigue, there is office gossip and town gossip. In *Hedda Gabler* the whole town already knows at ten o'clock in the morning that Ejlert Lövborg was drunk again the night before. In *An Enemy of the People* and in *Pillars of Society* gossip is actually the main theme: "What will the printer think, what will the judge say, and what will the headmaster suppose?" Under such conditions one loses so much time by these senseless vexations that a man is easily led to think he has wasted his whole life. There is in *Peer Gynt* a moving scene in which the old man's entire unlived life, his unthought thoughts, his unspoken words, his unshed tears, his unaccomplished deeds hover around him reproachfully and sorrowfully. Before these people begin to suffer in such circumstances, they have nearly all experienced a confused, almost dreamlike childhood in a kind of enchanted forest from which they emerge insatiably homesick and peculiarly insulated, like Parzival riding out into the world dressed as a fool and with the experience of a small child. This childhood of Parzival in the forest of Brezilian has always had some great symbolical significance for me. This growing up in a twilit world of solitude, the dreamlike questions about God and the world, answered by a mother's childlike, dreamlike answer, all this is in reality a typical growing-up in the twilit and mysteriously confused atmosphere of a parental home, where all dimensions seem distorted, all things appear stylized. For children's eyes give

Hugo von Hofmannsthal 85

things a form which we strive in vain to re-
capture. Commonplace events become fabulous or heroic, in the same way that dread,
fever, or genius transform them. In just
such a wood as Brezilian, which is a doll's
house, they all grew up: Nora and Hedda
with ailing and eccentric fathers; Hjalmar
with hysterical women, the aunts; Julian
in the bad air of a Byzantine monastery;
Peer Gynt with his fantastic, half-mad
mother, and so on. That childhood left them
with something peculiarly dreamlike; they
always appear to be thinking about something other than what they are talking
about; they are all poets, or, more correctly,
sensitive dilettantes. They have much in
common with the Emperor Nero and with
Don Quixote; for they also wish to trans-
pose fiction into life, irrespective of whether
it is their own invention or adopted by
them. A few have resigned themselves to
no longer believing in the miraculous thing
that was to come from without. They believe in the infinite capacity for the miraculous in man: they believe in the creative,
transfiguring, ennobling power of pain.
This is one of the favourite items in Henrik
Ibsen's personal faith: he believes that
something miraculous comes to life in
human beings when they meet grave difficulties. . . .

They are also given to playing with
palpable, living words, which is so characteristic of the poet: certain words appear to
have quite a different meaning for them
than they have for ordinary people; they
pronounce them with their own special
intonation, half in pleasure, half in dread,
like sacred incantations. They use amongst
themselves quotations and familiar phrases,
even when they do not happen to be vain
sophists like the Emperor Julian, who is
always quoting himself. They are also
deeply concerned about their exits: they
love an organized death; even if they do
not sink down with quotations from Seneca,
like the princes in an earlier Shakespeare,
a slight pose belongs to the situation. I am
reminded of the sad words of a young girl

from a good family who, a few days before
her death, said with an elegant smile,
"Après tout, le suicide calme, c'est la seule
chose bien aristocratique qui nous reste."
Hedda might almost have said that, or Dr.
Rank; nor does little Hedwig die naïvely.
And Julian, after a life full of disappoint-
ments, cannot die without thinking of the
effect. "See this black water," he says to
his friend, "do you think that if I were
to disappear without trace from the face of
the earth, and if my body were not found
anywhere and no one knew where I was—
do you not think the tale might spread that
Hermes had come and carried me away,
and I had been taken up into the company
of the Gods?"

How closely we here approach the manner of Nero, that real and very living Nero
whom Renan has formed from the details
of Petronius, of Suetonius, and of the
Apocalypse: a mediocre artist in whose
head Bacchus and Sardanapalus, Ninus and
Priam, Troy and Babylon, Homer and the
insipid verses of his contemporaries swirl
in confusion, a conceited virtuoso who
makes the groundlings tremble and himself
trembles at them, a witty dilettante who
gazes upon his mother's dead body through
an emerald lens with aesthetic pleasure,
praising here, censuring there, and to whom
nothing but literary reminiscences occur in
his own hour of death. He remembers that
he acted parts in which he portrayed parri-
cides and princes reduced to beggary, and
remarks that he is now playing all this on
his own account, and he declaims the words
of Oedipus:

"Wife and Mother and Father bid me die!"

Then he speaks Greek, composes verse,
until the sound is heard of approaching
horsemen, who are to capture him alive.
Then he cries,

"The dull sound of galloping horses deafens my
ears!"

and "in beauty" he receives the death-blow
from a slave who thrusts the dagger.

It is indeed not surprising that there is such affinity between this Nero and that Julian; they are both in the same degree self-portraits of their authors, two brilliant philosophers of the nineteenth century.

Nero's education in the rhetorical school of the affected Seneca, that virtuoso of imitation, has much in common with our own; and all those literary dilettantes in Ibsen's plays might well have written in their diaries those splendid words that Seneca spoke about his own time, "Literarum intemperantia laboramus," with this comment, "I have never been carried away by my life, I lacked the immediacy of experience, and it was so petty that in order to give it some interest I had to embellish it with witty constructions, with artificial antitheses and nuances." This decorating of everyday life, this quaintly beautiful way of life which (in its terminology at least) resembles that of Protestant devotional books, this stern, all-absorbing concentration on the "one necessity," this hard and harsh emphasis on the duties towards oneself—these things imply (depending on the particular characters involved) two ultimate conceptions of the problems of life. One is symbolic self-isolation, the necessity imposed by the nerves of creating an abyss on all sides, the solitary stand of the Enemy of the People, the growing loneliness at Rosmersholm, the flight of Nora into the night. The alternative is to remain in life and move among men, but as a secret master, to whom all others are objects, batteries of moods, pieces of furniture, devices that illumine, that amuse, that provoke or move. This is the way Helmer treats his wife and his friend Dr. Rank. His wife is a toy, a pretty and elegant doll, whom he takes to a party, lets dance the tarantella; then he collects the compliments and takes her away again, whether she likes it or not. And when his friend hides himself away in order to die quietly like a wounded animal, he says: "Pity, for his suffering and his loneliness seemed almost to provide a beautiful background of dark cloud to the sunshine of our lives." Still more delightful, however, is the passage in another play where a group of three people regard each other in turn as a thing for evoking a mood: I refer to the sick sculptor Lyngstrand and the two young girls, stepdaughters of the Lady from the Sea. The man, ill beyond hope, speaks about his impending journey to Italy and obtains a promise from the elder of the two girls that she will constantly direct her thoughts away from her poor, monotonous existence to him. Why? "Well, you see," he says, "just to know that somewhere in the world some young woman, gentle and quiet, is secretly dreaming of one. . . ." He finds this tremendously "thrilling."

But at the same time he is not really interested in her, but in the younger sister, an adolescent and very wise little person. "When I come back," he tells her, "you will be just about as old as your sister is now. Perhaps then you will look as she does now. Perhaps you will then, so to speak, be both yourself and her in one person. . . ." Hilda toys with the idea that the man who tells her all this will never return, because she knows that he must die. This flirtation at the gates of death gives a very particular pleasure. She asks him how she would look in black, completely in black, with a black ruffle around her neck and with black gloves. . . .

"Like a young, beautiful widow in mourning, you mean?"

"Yes," she says, "or like a young bride in mourning."

She in her turn finds *that* thought tremendously thrilling.

These resigned egoists like Hjalmar, Helmer, and Hilda, and the pathetically isolated ones such as Stockmann or Nora, are to my mind only phases of one and the same inner experience, and these different people are nothing more than the one Ibsenist creature in various stages of development. All Ibsen's characters represent simply a ladder of states of mind, all of which Julian (to take but one example of them) has in embryo and which he lives through. In each play one idea, or rather one aspect of a great fundamental problem, is specially emphasized and followed through logically in the French manner.

And the fundamental problem is, I believe, always the same essentially undramatic one: how does the Ibsenist creature, the artistic egoist, the sensitive dilettante with abundant capacity for self-observation, with little will power and a great yearning for beauty and innocence, how does this being conduct itself in life?

What if one wants to bind it and force it, and it is of a weak and helpless disposition?—Nora.

Or if one wants to force it when it is of a strong and arrogant disposition?—Stockmann.

Or if it is allowed freedom and the torment of choice?—The Lady from the Sea.

Or it is poor and would have social obligations?—Hjalmar.

Or it has all the power in the world?—Julian.

Or it is incurably ill?—Oswald Alving.

Or it has had a too intense upbringing?—Hedda.

I think the answer is very simple. It really does not belong among people and cannot make anything of life. Because of this it will sometimes die: for example Julian, Rosmer, Hedda. Or it "sets itself apart," which is practically the same: Nora, Stockmann. Or it lives on, solitary among people, selfishly regarding itself as their secret master: Hjalmar, Helmer, Hilda . . . in proud resignation and bleak disappointment, a fragile, artificial existence.

Meanwhile *The Master Builder* has appeared—a strange mixture of allegory and real-life description. Like those lights that peasant children put in hollow pumpkins at night and which shine through the thin orange pulp, so the allegorical meaning here shines through hollowed-out, lifelike dolls. The whole play has been interpreted ingeniously and certainly not incorrectly as a symbolic representation of Ibsen's inner development, of his attitude as an artist to God, to others, and to himself. The artist, the great master builder, stands between the two kings of *The Pretenders*. For with Ibsen, kings are also master builders, and master builders kings; or both are poets, royal master builders of souls. Master builder Solness therefore stands between King Haakon and King Skule. He has the daemonic luck of the one, and is torn by doubts, like the other. He has the "ingenium," the innate sense of vocation, the status of master builder by the grace of God, the right and the duty to win through, like Haakon, the born king, "the one with the kingly thought"; he also has the limitations, fears, pangs of conscience, and craving for power and facility in life, like King Skule, who has no right to be king. The artist, seen from within, looks like these kings and master builders; and Hjalmar and Julian are caricatures of him. Around the creative artist is life, exacting, scornful, confusing. Thus Princess Hilda confronts the vacillating master builder. She is little Hilda, stepdaughter of the Lady from the Sea, now grown up. The master builder once promised her a kingdom, and now she comes to claim it. If he is a born king, this must be quite easy for him. If not, he must simply perish as a result. And that would be tremendously thrilling. Her kingdom lies, like that of Nora and Hedda, in the realm of the miraculous—where one is overcome by dizziness, where one is seized by a strange power and carried away. He too has this yearning in his soul to stand on high towers, where in the wind and in the dusky loneliness it is uneasily beautiful, where one talks to God and where one can fall headlong to one's death. But he is not proof against giddiness; he goes in dread of himself, in dread of fortune, in dread of life, mysterious life in its entirety. He is also drawn to Hilda by dread, a peculiarly alluring fear, the awe felt by the artist for nature, for the merciless, daemonic, sphinx-like qualities inherent in woman, the mystic

fear of youth. For youth has something un-
canny about it, an intoxicating and dangerous breath of life which is mysterious and
disquieting. Everything problematical in
him, every repressed mystic quality in him,
is roused by her touch. In Hilda he meets
himself, he demands a miracle of himself,
he wants to force it out of himself, and at
the same time watch and feel the awe "when
life takes hold of a man and makes him the
stuff of poetry." At this point he falls to
his death.

I do not think that this partly ingenious
and partly frivolous way of pulling Ibsen's
plays apart and shaking them up together
can really harm them. One simply cannot
wander amidst them as among real people
in the living air, as one can in Shakespeare's
world, from the market through the court-
yard into the king's private chapel and
thence past the noisy banquet down the
stairs, past the guardroom, the tavern, the
magistrate's house, the crossroads, the
churchyard . . . but one traverses the rich
and silent soul of a prodigious man, with
moonlight, fantastic shadows, wafting
winds, and black lakes—silent mirrors in
which one recognizes oneself, enormously
enlarged and strangely and beautifully
transformed.

Una Ellis-Fermor

Ibsen and Shakespeare as Dramatic Artists

As THE world comes to understand better something of the greatness of Ibsen as a dramatic artist, we realise that his art stands by itself, not only, as does that of every great poet, by the impress of his individuality, but because he attempts in drama something which is without precise counterpart in the work of the major dramatists who are his peers. Aeschylus, Sophocles, Euripides and Shakespeare are all poetic dramatists and their art is not only expressed but conceived in terms of poetry; the language of poetry, charged with imagery, and the verbal music which is a part of their verse are both integral to their conception and inseparable from the form of the whole play. But Ibsen during much of his career wrote prose and the dramatic mode of some of his noblest plays is determined by or dictates the prose vehicle, just as theirs were determined by or dictated the vehicle of poetry. He chose, that is to say, the mode which is associated primarily with statement, with description, with argument, with philosophical thought; not that which is associated with poetic experience. He chose to be what we may perhaps call a philosopher-dramatist.

Now here is something of a paradox, for the nature of drama seems, so far as we can judge, to demand a complete concealment of the artist's self, his beliefs and his ideas, a loss of his personality in those of the people he creates; while they may have thoughts and opinions, may criticise and interpret the world in which he presents them, he must not. His function is to create an image of a world, not to describe, explain or analyse it. And this function determines the mode of his writing also, for, just as the nature of drama forbids the dramatist to state his own interpretation of man's life or destiny, so does it also forbid him to describe his characters or cause them, except in special cases, to describe themselves. The other four great dramatists whom we have named his peers lead us into understanding of characters and events by awakening in us a profound imaginative sympathy with these characters and these events; so profound that often we cannot express in words what we have apprehended in the depths of our minds. We learn from these plays as we do from life, at half-unawares, by unrecorded impressions and by knowledge hidden from our conscious thought. For they are in truth an image of life and not a sermon, however noble, upon life's issues. That wise critic, Maurice Morgann, said, nearly two hundred years ago, that Shakespeare had "contrived to make secret impressions upon us," and the longer we study the work of Shakespeare the more deeply are we convinced that it is by these secret impressions that we guide ourselves in our interpretation of his plays.

Here then is a contrast, seemingly fundamental, between the poetic, evocative mode of Shakespeare and the way in which Ibsen, in certain of the plays written after 1875, presents for our consideration problems whose nature he defines for us and whose importance he illuminates simultaneously by debates between characters and selection and juxtaposition of episodes which themselves approximate to argument. And so, at the end of a careful study of, say, *Pillars of the Community*, we know or

From *Shakespeare the Dramatist*, ed. Kenneth Muir, Methuen, London, 1961; first published in *Edda*, Oslo, 1956. Reprinted by permission.

ought to know something of what Ibsen thought about truth and lies in public life and those of us who have studied his work through many years find it comparatively easy to agree upon his reading of life and upon his scale of values. At least we know that truth, in public and private life, truth in the heart, was a thing he valued so highly that he testified to its virtue directly or indirectly in nearly every play he wrote and that, close to it and inseparably associated with it in his work, we find certain other great values: freedom, love, responsibility. But no man has yet been able to say what Shakespeare thought of life, though many have tried and by many roads. All we can certainly say is that whatever we know he knew before us; that he is the eternal companion of our experience. And that means that for each of us he is something different.

Now here we have clearly a sundering difference between Shakespeare and Ibsen in their initial conception of their art, in that vision of a portion of life which constitutes the inspiration of a play. And we shall not be surprised then to find that Shakespeare reveals a character, say that of Ophelia, by means of hints that cannot be understood until we bring to bear upon them the witness of the whole play and that he does something very like that with the widely different character of, for instance, Coriolanus. These are both unable to express their underlying selves in speech and action, the one because she is emotionally inarticulate, the other, though eloquent, because he so profoundly misunderstands himself that we only discover his hidden nature by the aid of Shakespeare's "secret impressions." Utterly unlike this is Ibsen's way with the character of, say, Karsten Bernick, whose self-knowledge is so nearly complete that he only with great difficulty shuts his eyes to the inference that follows from it. When once he has been forced to acknowledge this, he proves the extent of his self-knowledge by an analysis as lucid as a philosopher's. Utterly unlike Shakespeare's

mode, but again illustrative of his own, is that of a host of other thoughtful men and women in Ibsen's plays who have won self-knowledge at the conscious, intellectual level and are themselves our guides in the interpretation of their lives: Nora Helmer, Mrs. Alving, Halvard Solness. They are all, in a wide sense of the term, philosophers, just as is their creator.

And in the same way we may contrast the seemingly loose, evocative technique of Shakespeare's structure in *Macbeth* with that of Ibsen in *Pillars of the Community, A Doll's House, An Enemy of the People, The Wild Duck, Hedda Gabler*. In *Macbeth* we are carried forward by great leaps of the imagination from event to event, their psychological significance determining Shakespeare's instinctive selection and their evocative power such that we too pass from one to the other with instinctive understanding of their hidden relation and their inevitable result. In clear contrast stands the exquisite articulation of Ibsen's plotting, which demonstrates, with compelling logic, the inevitable path of cause and consequence.

All this is clear enough and has so long been recognised that I do not propose to dwell upon it, but rather, if I may, to attempt to correct the balance of some of our assumptions. For I think, and I speak now chiefly of English criticism and of the conclusions accepted by lovers of Ibsen in my own country, that we at one time laid undue emphasis on this particular group of his plays and that this still results in an interpretation of Ibsen which tends to look too steadily at the philosopher in him and too seldom at the poet. I should like to suggest that we may find in Ibsen too the evocative mode of the great poetic dramatist, and that, not merely where, as in *Peer Gynt*, we cannot fail to see it, but also in those very prose plays where we have taken too little thought of it. The task of writing what is virtually poetic drama in the mood and manner of prose was one of such difficulty that we may, without disrespect, say that Ibsen did not at once achieve it. That he did achieve it, and in somewhat the same terms as Shakespeare, and that we can perhaps indicate some stages in his progress towards it, is the suggestion that I should like to make.

I will not stay now to substantiate what I have said of the group of prose plays that begin with *Pillars of the Community,* but will ask for a measure of agreement when I say that in the greater part of most of them we find a dramatist who differs widely from Sophocles and Shakespeare, one whose method is essentially demonstrative, whose major characters are often self-explanatory and whose structure is often itself an argument as cogent as a logical cantena.[1] Nevertheless, even in these plays, the two modes can be found side by side, hints of this duality being discernible as early as *Pillars of the Community.* But at the height of his power, in the final group of plays, evocation and not demonstration controls both the revelation of character and the unfolding of event that constitutes plot. We find in *Ghosts* a clear instance of the double process and in *Rosmersholm* a supreme revelation of evocative technique in prose drama.

We shall agree, I think, in saying that the structure of *Ghosts* is one of the most beautiful pieces of formal art to be found in drama. Perhaps the most interesting aspect of this structure is to be found in the grouping of the characters, which in turn determines the logic of event. Some critics nowadays like to call this the spatial aspect of a play; it may be thought of as a picture and, if we adopt Lessing's convenient distinction, as static in time and extended in space. In studying it we consider the characters not primarily in terms of their experience, but in terms of the illumination we receive from their juxtaposition and their relative positions in the composition. Looked at like this, *Ghosts* may be seen as a simple, but massive group of statuary, in which the characters balance each other in respect of the central theme or thought to the definition of which they all contribute; the five are so selected that each brings to the central idea of the play one part of the final, composite effect. The dead hand of convention and duty has subdued to its purposes Pastor Manders, who has thus become its vehicle and its exponent, but it has driven Mrs. Alving to rebellion and so to emancipation of thought. Modifying the contrasted positions of these two, are three others who show the workings of that same compulsion upon related, yet differing, minds and characters. Each of these three provides a variation on the theme and in representative proportions: Regine has rebelled without thought or heart-searching and has suffered the degeneration that comes of rejecting the good and the bad alike in a given social code; her "father," Engstrand, as immoral as she but more shrewd, has cunningly observed the workings of the system and found his account in playing upon its victims; Osvald has escaped psychological harm only to be destroyed by the physical consequences from which nothing could save him. Each of the five bears direct or indirect testimony to the weight of this dead hand and their relationship demonstrates the operation of the curse; a Laokoon group of figures still imprisoned or too late emancipated to maintain valid life.

With this image of the play in mind, we can observe Ibsen's method in more detail. In the first place, each character is so related to the theme of his play that whichever one we study we still have in view those others whose functions are complementary to its function, who depend upon it for their balance as it depends on them for its. And, in the second, the structure of the whole, with its living tension, is itself an argument, a demonstration of the tragic effects of the suppression of truth and free-

[1] This is not, of course, to confuse Ibsen's technique or mode with that in which the characters are the mouthpieces, not of their own knowledge but of the dramatist's, and where the movement of the plot is less that of cogent argument than of the punctual revolutions of a machine.

dom in the characters and fates of this compact and closely welded group of figures.

Ibsen, as we have said, begins his grouping with the figures of Manders and Mrs. Alving, in frank though not at first unfriendly opposition at the centre of the play: Manders, a man moulded by slavery to convention and totally unaware of the evil of this, since for him the laws of custom have taken the place of honest thought and opinion, a man readily persuaded that evil is good and good evil, provided only that the conventions of his time and place give their assent: Mrs. Alving, a woman who has outgrown false standards as completely as Manders has accepted them, who has discarded the sentimentality and insincerity in which both he and she had been reared and has learned through bitterness and self-discipline to speak the truth in her heart; who has developed to the point at which she can understand and repudiate shams and deceits, whether in Manders or in a society which is solidly against her. His distinction thus made manifest, his two central positions thus defined, Ibsen proceeds with strength and economy to support them by the other three—we might almost say by the other four—characters; Osvald, who has lived in and experienced the healthy world in which work and living are joyous things and has recognised its normality without going through a mental crisis to win that recognition; Regine, his half-sister, who has similar instincts, made crude, coarse and rebellious in part by her own heritage, but in part also by her life in a society which condemns and shrinks from them; Engstrand, the embodiment of servility and cunning fostered by falsehoods, traditions, and lies. Finally, there is the spirit of the dead Captain Alving, who can hardly in fairness be left out of the character list. At the beginning of the play, something of a mystery, his relation to the central theme is undefined, but his character and conduct receive three different interpretations before we uncover the original man and with

that final uncovering the last touch is put to the tragic argument implicit in the structure of this Laokoon group.

So much for the spatial aspect of this play. If this image has served to illuminate in any degree the cogency of the structure, the way in which Ibsen has made of the very juxtaposition of these characters an argument upon the central theme, it has served its purpose. But the temporal aspect of the structure, the movement of events through time (the other half of Lessing's convenient distinction), this again offers an elucidation of the idea Ibsen is concerned to convey. The nature of "duty" dictated by the dead hand of the past is gradually illuminated by the emergence of an alternative conception of man's destiny as the theme of joy is gradually defined by those charged with the attack upon the "ghosts" of conventions and lies. The forward movement of the action is inevitable, with the inevitableness of that which is perfectly natural. Mrs. Alving and Manders have known each other for a quarter of a century; we recognise from the first that they have a store of memories which they now call up and now evade. It is therefore natural that they should discuss their past and inevitable that discussion should end explosively, with wreck and ruin and revelation that disclose the past and precipitate the future; the logic is flawless that drives us step by step to the conclusion. Here again, in the movement of event no less than in the essential apposition of the figures, it is character that serves the theme. Thus the great scenes in which Mrs. Alving and Pastor Manders interpret to themselves and to us the central idea and the meaning of the action have many simultaneous functions, illuminating the past, so that we see it reaching forward to strangle the present, revealing first Manders's then Mrs. Alving's interpretation of all that had happened in the recent history of the fated house of Alving, stripping away the deception, exposing his self-deception. It brings into clear and implacable contrast the two interpretations of life, of the relation of the individual to society and even more of the true organization of society itself. Moreover, it does this with the intensity that grows out of tragic passion and the memory of passion—just how much, we gradually discover as the play goes on—and it has the concentration of a dramatic crisis combined with the lucidity of Ibsen's conversational analyses in *Pillars of the Community* and in *A Doll's House*. This can only be done by setting the events far enough in the past for thought to have matured and cleared for Mrs. Alving and hardened and petrified for Manders, so that the characters speak with absolute certainty of their meaning, the passion stirring and deepening their thought but not confusing it.

But is there perhaps something that we have passed by in describing the compulsive logic of the character-grouping and of the ordered sequence of events? In describing, that is, the demonstrative and argumentative functions of the structure of this play, those aspects of its form that mark it as the work of a philosopher-dramatist? I think there is and that we shall find in Ibsen's treatment of one character and in part of his treatment of another something that we first apprehend by the aid of intimations closely akin to the "secret impressions" of the mode of evocative drama. To put it paradoxically there are six additional characters in this play, all of whom are revealed by technique more profoundly evocative than that of the later Jean Jacques Bernard and the *Théâtre de Silence*. In studying the revelation of these characters we find ourselves in the presence of the dramatist who was later, in *Rosmersholm*, to create a great part of his play out of hints, silences and intimations.

Mrs. Alving changes in the course of the play. At the beginning, we might expect her to be a static character, one who had made terms finally with life and would maintain her position to the end. But, and this is one of the triumphs of Ibsen's art, when the explosions and upheavals of the second and third acts shatter her world, she responds to them not by a hardening rigidity, but by further exploration and discovery. The principle of growth is still at work in her; she is a living spirit still. We watch her evolve under our eyes from the clear-sighted, unsentimental woman we first met into one who can see not merely that "duty" has poisoned her life, sacrificed her to a lie and starved her of reality, but that she herself has contributed to her own tragedy. Reared in terms of duty and obligation, she in her turn had starved the joy of life in another person, in the husband whom nature had endowed with that joy. She recognises this and admits it, making thereby a great stride forward into a larger freedom. Not for her to go through the remainder of her life, like the tragic figure of Mrs. Solness, reiterating miserably the phrase "It was only my duty." In this moment she comes within measurable distance of recognising another "duty," to joy, to gladness and to love, a duty akin to Wordsworth's "Stern daughter of the voice of God" of whom nevertheless he could also say "Nor know we anything so fair As is the smile upon thy face."

But this discovery makes us pause, precisely as certain discoveries about Ophelia or Coriolanus make us pause, to reconsider in its light something we had perhaps passed over. The principle of growth is still alive in her. Then the principle of growth must have been in her from the beginning and there must be a longer history of its working than that contained in the events of the play. When we see that, we see suddenly that Ibsen has revealed to us not two phases of Mrs. Alving's spiritual growth but five, all of them necessary to our understanding of her but three of them belonging to the distant past of the play and evoked by touches, by hints, by implications. Long ago there had been a credulous and romantic girl, the untrained, uneducated child of a sterile upper-class society, who committed her first deadly sin by making a marriage that betrayed her own instincts and desires. (For Ibsen, here as always, this crime must be expiated by repentance and tears.) This is the first Mrs. Alving, the woman who, coerced by those set in authority over her, had married a rich man whom she did not love instead of the poor pastor whom she did. The next, I fancy, is the woman who, recoiling from the vices she had helped to drive him to, left her husband, only to be shepherded back into the path of "duty." Into the path of duty, and by Manders, but not into the path of love by her own will. From this there slowly evolved the strong, hard, dominating woman, the "femme maîtrise," who set herself to save the family name for her son by thrusting this husband still further out of her life, putting all the force of her will to building for him a false reputation of nobility. From this in turn evolved the woman, clear-sighted but still unpitying, whom we meet at the beginning of the play. In the third phase we catch glimpses of a dangerous likeness to Gunhild Borkman, but her love for her son, unlike Gunhild's, had been selfless and unpossessive and through it she was suffered to work out her salvation. Five characters, instead of one. These are the things that enrich a play and enrich it with the infinite extensions of the poetic imagination.

But Ibsen the evocative poet has not done with us yet. He has still in reserve Captain Alving—one had better say at once three Captain Alvings. The dead captain cannot appear in the play; but his ghost is one of the most powerful of those that walk. Beside his continual half-seen presence, the paradoxical absent figures of the Théâtre de Silence become dim shadows. We discover him in reverse, as we discover much in Rosmersholm, beginning with the nearest appearance and guided gradually to hints of the earlier and of the underlying reality. First comes the good citizen, the man of philanthropic activities that Manders and general opinion recognise, the man to whose noble life and services the memorial is to be unveiled. Then follows the drunken, worn-out rake that Mrs. Alving shows us— the man who had only been kept from dis-

gracing his name by being hidden in the background, while his wife built up the fiction of his noble philanthropic activities by doing the work herself. And finally we discover the man that she, illuminated by his own son Osvald, sees for the first time at the end, a man whose love of life had been poisoned, thwarted and debased by living in a society which saw nothing but evil in that joy.

If we perceive this in Ghosts, we are I think prepared to recognise here a play which has two strains, the philosopher-dramatist designing the great argument of the central theme and dedicating to its demonstration the character-grouping and progressive definition of the ideas and the poet-dramatist so widening the implications of his characters' experience that we find ourselves in the presence of poetic drama, of the creative and evocative mode.

Now it is my belief that in the later plays, especially in those from The Wild Duck onwards, this latter mode gradually prevails over the first; that the poet of Peer Gynt slowly resumes the mastery over philosopher, social critic and satirist. Nothing could alter the fact that Ibsen had written the prose plays, just as nothing in Milton's later poetic career could wipe out the effects of his long digression into prose-writing between Comus and Paradise Lost. A "born poet" does now and then fall "upon an age of prose"; not an age in which poetry is not written, but an age in which it is not lived, an age, that is, in which the matter of men's experience, the habit of their thought and the language they exchange seem all to be prosaic, argumentative or matter-of-fact. In such an age, the drama, mirroring its mood, will tend to divide upon this very issue, associating romantic subject with poetic vehicle and the interpretation of familiar life with the prose vehicle and the prosaic mood. Nevertheless the mood of that age must enter the poet's mind as a part of his experience and, if he continues to write, it will partly determine the form of his communication. No other way, no other course of development, is possible for him, for, by the nature of his function, he cannot either exclude experience or set deliberate limits to the process of communication. But what the great poet may yet do is to transmute the experience he must not reject, the forms he must necessarily use and so, ultimately, the age itself, into the prose of whose life and thought he had fallen. There greets us at this point one of those paradoxes that illuminate the way of the artist; for the life that, as an artist, he had seemed to lose, is then restored to him, a greater life than he could have reached without the assimilation and transmutation of the obstinate, intransigent, alien prose of the world. It is a commonplace of criticism to say that without the religious and political tracts on which Milton spent his middle years, there would have been no Conclave in Hell. It is equally certain that without the long preoccupation with moral issues, practical, and at least in part critical and philosophical, Ibsen would not have emerged where he did in *The Wild Duck*. In the interval since *The Pretenders* (and even in that play the process was already beginning), he has taken into his imagination the moral habit of his age, its preoccupation, genuine or hypocritical, with issues that are in essence social and ethical, as Milton assimilated political and religious controversy. And because he is of major stature, he too at length transmutes the experience into a War in Heaven, creating a mode of communication in which the mental habits of the men of his time can find full expression, in drama which can reach the grand scale of poetry precisely because it has neither denied them nor obeyed them. He has made a new art, a new kind of drama, because instead of accepting as his material the interpretation his contemporaries made of themselves and as his mode the habit of their thinking, he has subdued them and it, transferring their warfare from counting-houses and stove-heated villas to the plains of eternity. And this done, he too, like Milton, fulfilled also the third condition, for he transmuted in turn the habit and the thinking of that age which had threatened to subdue him, bringing back to Europe a drama urgent and alive, reaching the minds of men as only a living drama could still reach them.

Now Shakespeare's way was different, since his age and his men were predominantly neither moral, political nor religious but human and explorers of human life. But the ends of the two dramatists are alike, for they converge in poetry, which is the destiny of drama. Ibsen could not have followed the poetic mode continuously through his middle phases, for to have done so would have been to reject the material immediately about him, that habit of life which he must work in and work upon if his art were to reach the common roots of that and of all other ways of life. But precisely because of this his last plays fulfil, in terms of his own world, the destiny of drama; they are prophetic and creative because, beneath their seemingly prosaic demeanour, they are poetic and evocative. He found European drama at its best accomplished, critical, observant, and entertaining; he left it restored to its ancient mastery of men's souls.

Now the final phase of this is to be seen in the late plays. But, as I have suggested, the process by which it was achieved may in part be guessed at when we look at those of an earlier date in which Ibsen "fell," in a sense not strictly implicit in Matthew Arnold's, upon his "age of prose." I have confined my hints in speaking of *Ghosts* to purely technical questions and to a special aspect of technique, that of the mode of writing. There is not time for more (nor time indeed for this, in any proper fullness) but I am convinced that what we may there see in a single aspect of his craft represents something that is characteristic also of the whole field of his content, the shaping of his material, the underlying thought, and his apprehension of life. And if we now turn to the later plays it will be again to look at this aspect of the technique, leaving it, as before, to represent in miniature the poet's mind.

Ibsen works still, in this later phase, in terms of the habits of thought that the men of his age imposed upon themselves, but the prosaic demeanour, the argumentative or philosophical elucidation, belongs now to his characters alone and no longer in part to their creator. His way now is to reveal to us by hints and suggestions a hidden self at variance with the surface, a self unknown to or unacknowledged by the conscious, active mind of the character. Here is again the poetic and evocative mode that we saw in *Ghosts;* our imaginations act upon these hints to reinterpret the characters' judgements of themselves and of each other. The conversation of Hedda Gabler, focussed though it is upon her tastes, her views, her opinions, tells us hardly anything of her inner experience, so that there have been readers whom her suicide has taken by surprise. But this smooth mask, the smoother for seeming to declare itself openly, is momentarily broken by instants of self-revelation (the threat to burn off Thea's hair, the actual burning of her "child") which, because of the sudden glimpse of molten passion at work beneath, reveal at once the danger, the significance and the tragedy of the mask. To work thus, to contradict by a single touch the evidence that a character has painfully built up throughout the play, is to work in the way of Shakespeare with Ophelia or Coriolanus; it is the technique of evocation, not of statement. In the same way we are led to divine the past deeds and experiences of characters, not by their own elucidation of them, but by their fumbling approaches to self-discovery or by those touches of contradiction which reinterpret an apparently self-evident picture. Thea, Ellida, Solness, Ella Rentheim and Gunhild Borkman, all in their different ways lay trembling or uncertain hands upon clues that lead them back through their past to an understanding that we discover with them and, like them, imperfectly. General Gabler, though less often

spoken of, is closer to our elbow even than Captain Alving. The incidents in *Rosmersholm* fall half fortuitously, more nearly as do the events of *Macbeth;* they either have no logical inevitability, or if they have, that is not what we notice; in themselves they are nothing, their function is to provoke continuing reflection in us and in the characters. In *Little Eyolf* it is the slender hints, the almost invisible references, that reveal the strength of the compulsions determining the relationship of the four central characters, and stifling in different ways the life of each. In *John Gabriel Borkman* the in-driven natures of the older people lead them to talk at length and without social prevarication about their past tragedies and their schemes for the future. But by a terrible irony Ibsen reveals the incompatibility not merely of these intentions but of the interpretations themselves, so that each reading of the past except Ella's and all their purposes with the future become unreal to the measure of their contradiction of each other, while, from this mixture of congruence and conflict, reality, if we can read it, is evoked.

Rosmersholm is the first play in which supreme achievement in this kind is revealed and the distinctive marks of the late manner are already clear. The plot whose events are the findings brought back from the exploration and revaluation of the past; the profound concern with the inner experience of the mind and with the processes of its self-discovery; the swift, elliptic dialogue at moments of high tension; all these belong to the last phase of Ibsen's writing and are related more or less closely to those parts of the middle plays in which we traced the poetic mode alongside the critical and philosophic. But there are certain advances and variations, here and in the plays that follow, which show that now the poetic mode has prevailed over the philosophic. A long history of mingled outward and inward event, of interacting deeds and decisions, lies behind this play, as behind *Ghosts.* But it is no longer revealed so much by open discussion and analysis as by slight and almost secret impressions. The years before its opening scene might have furnished material for an Elizabethan domestic tragedy. But the substance of this play is the recollection of such a history, its reassessment in terms of the culminating phase of Rebekka's love, and it is to this exploration that the slight and colourless events of the outward drama prompt her. She works her way backwards under their stimulus, tracing her deeds to their sources, illuminating both deed and motive by her new realisation of nobility and love and reinterpreting her present duty by the guidance of this understanding. The character-grouping again, which may seem unchanged, in fact no longer suggests the sculptured image of a theme. It is still a small group of people isolated and closely related, but they are no longer united by their suffering at the hands of a common fate. The close relationship is only accidental; a matter of place and time and physical proximity.

At the centre of the group is the House of Rosmer revealed in John Rosmer, its last descendant, a man of a sensitive and noble imagination, limited in action by his position, but not mentally inactive. The strong but cruder natures of the earlier Rebekka and the Kroll of the time of the play, who destroy between them the peace of his mind but not its lofty self-discipline, reveal by the urgency of their purposes the still and contemplative nature of his. They are in turn illuminated by the essentially unimaginative Brendel, in whom rhetoric has dissipated purpose, and by Mortensgaard, in whom the disciplined purpose of expediency has quenched alike passion and vision. None of these could be modified without destroying the effect of the others; the colour of each is intimately dependent upon contrast with and reflection from the colours of all the rest. To all these, the matter-of-fact figure of Mrs. Helseth serves as a background, as a reminder of a normal world of unaspiring and unthwarted beings cheerfully un-

touched by the Rosmer view of life. But these minds are in fact widely separated, half-hostile explorers making partial and momentary contact in the unknown country of the past. The loneliness of self-examination and self-discovery surrounds them, leaving them to guess at each other's positions, hiding them often when they try to approach. And in this lonely exploration we too must discover them by hints as much as by plain revelation, and sometimes by hints that contradict what had seemed to be demonstrable evidence.

In fact, such a subject, with its "reminiscential evocation," demands a subtle cross-lighting of the characters, so that they may in their turn illuminate each other and the relations between them. For their function is not to demonstrate a theme (though they do in fact discuss many), but to give us a picture of the changing, shifting vicissitudes of the human soul, of its bewildered pilgrimage and, it may be, of its final illumination. To the implications of such plays, whether in terms of character or of event, there is no limit, for their imaginative dimensions reach as far as the thought that they evoke can travel. They have no logic except the logic of poetry, and the mode of poetry has no limitations. We have come a long way from the period of the writing of *Peer Gynt*, but it is clear that, by obscure or it may be devious ways, Ibsen's art has found its way back to and now moves surely in the paths of poetry and power.

One minor but distinctive manifestation of the evocative mode in Ibsen's drama is to be found in the elliptic dialogue at moments of high tension which, passing over from the great poetic period, becomes more and more frequent in the late plays. This technique in dialogue, so evidently akin to the allusive, evocative revelation of plot and character in these same plays, is to be seen most clearly in the final passages. Here, in *Peer Gynt*, in *Rosmersholm*, in *When We Dead Awaken* and in only less degree in *Brand* and *Little Eyolf*, the resolution of the play is revealed in each case in a passage of dialogue so wholly dependent upon suggestion and the overtones of speech as to be bewildering or almost unintelligible to a reader who has not understood the half-hidden implications in the rest of the play. Of them all, the most noble —and the most obscure to those who have not disposed their imaginations to listen to the evocative overtones—are perhaps the concluding passages of *Peer Gynt* and of *Rosmersholm*. The speeches are simple, brief fragments of utterance, spanning wide gulfs of thought; the two minds in each case seeming to read each other's thought almost without the help of words. The dialogue which reveals this communion of spirit indicates, as it were with touches and hints, the intent and crucial discoveries of two minds swiftly approaching the disclosure of an irradiating truth. No dramatic technique but that of the evocative mode can achieve such revelation as this and no imagination can follow it that has not submitted itself throughout the play to the mode of poetic thought. To describe in 'common words' what flashes from mind to mind between Peer and Solveig or between Rosmer and Rebekka requires several passages of somewhat halting and embarrassed prose. There are passages of dialogue in Shakespeare's plays that have the same quality and make the same demands upon our imaginations; they are to be found here and there too in the other Elizabethan dramatists and in the work of Aeschylus and of Sophocles. Wherever they appear they carry within them the note of high po-

etry and are the unfailing signs in drama of the evocative and poetic mode.

To what conclusions have these suggestions been pointing us? To the conclusion that Ibsen, by nature and destiny a poetic dramatist, was born into an age whose preoccupations and mental habits were alien to poetic drama because it had lost the habit of poetic life; that Ibsen's career as an artist reveals a gigantic struggle between his own innate poetic power and a way of life tending more and more to obscure poetic and imaginative reality; that Ibsen alone of all the dramatists of his century had the power to resolve this conflict and that that resolution could only be achieved by accepting the actual and the prosaic and transmuting it into the real and the poetic. The progress of this transmutation may, I think, be traced through his plays from *Peer Gynt* to *Rosmersholm* and its final achievement seen in the last seven plays. In the early stages of this conflict we find the paradoxical figure of the philosopher-dramatist, a major dramatic artist working in non-poetic material and using a partially unpoetic mode. In the final plays the mode is poetic (even if the vehicle is still prose) and the material has been subdued to the purposes of poetry. By a tentative comparison of a few aspects of his technique in two plays with the corresponding technique of Shakespeare we can, I think, perceive where his dramatic art separated from that of his predecessors, Aeschylus, Sophocles, Euripides and Shakespeare, and how and upon what terms it returned to the way of dramatic poetry.

Jens Arup

Narrative and Symbol in Ibsen

IBSEN occupies a rather peculiar position in modern criticism. He is valued for his economy and his technical brilliance, his subtlety and his essential honesty; and at the same time he is condemned for lack of precision, for vagueness of sentiment and portentous ambiguity of utterance. Ibsen's detractors complain of the lack of exactly those qualities for which he is most enthusiastically praised. The fundamental disagreement that exists does not prevent good critics from enlarging our appreciation of Ibsen's work, and I do not want to imply that Ibsen criticism is a barren field; but this disagreement is reflected in many fumbling productions, and it does also give a kind of sanction to entirely senseless interpretations.

Perhaps I may give an example: two years ago Miss Mary McCarthy wrote on Ibsen for the *Partisan Review*. She dealt at some length with *The Master Builder*, and stated dogmatically that this play is allegorical: the hero is Ibsen himself. Solness's buildings represent Ibsen's work, the churches corresponding to his early poetic plays, the dwelling houses to his realistic plays, and the house with the spire representing Ibsen's last "symbolic" plays. Naturally enough the critic found this subject inadequate to sustain the play—"strangely thin" is her phrase—and in short she dismissed the whole thing as an elaborately childish fabrication, mystification for its own sake. Perhaps it is ungallant to quote Miss McCarthy, who has written good criticism, when she is so obviously off her best form; but the point I want to make is that even Miss McCarthy would scarcely have had the authority to get this sort of twaddle into print if she had been dealing with anyone but Ibsen.

The trouble is that even those critics who do enlarge our understanding of Ibsen's work find it difficult to say exactly what a play like *The Master Builder* is about. Intellectually the play is baffling. It you want to regard it as a problem in algebra you can try, like a schoolboy who has not learnt his lesson, to guess at possible answers and see whether they will fit the formula—but it will not get you much further. The writers who do succeed in passing on some of their enthusiasm for the play, who convey a sense of its force and brilliance, do not often attempt to analyse it intellectually. The best critics are often actors, or writers with an actor's flair for feeling their way into a situation; for, although it is in some ways equivocal and ill-defined, *The Master Builder* is immediately accessible to the sympathetic imagination. When it is properly acted and staged, the play is extraordinarily effective; but then too many directors have managed to water it down fairly severely by trying to make it into an intellectual rather than a theatrical experience. It is the prevalence of attempts, by both critics and directors, to render Ibsen's last plays in intellectual terms that suggests the need for a new approach. I want to try to suggest the direction that a new assessment of these late plays might take; and for this purpose I want to discuss their structure, the way in which Ibsen organizes his often strange material so as to make the plays accessible to the audience.

Ibsen's earlier realistic plays are based

Reprinted with the author's permission from *The Listener*, British Broadcasting Corporation, London, 18 June 1959.

on the pattern he had learnt from Scribe, and even though they may have a complicated allusive texture they do not present any structural difficulties. But the later style developed naturally from the earlier one: stylistic devices that in the plays of his middle period were decorative and explanatory additions became the basic structural elements in his later work.

Nora's tarantella provides a good example of the earlier manner. In *A Doll's House* the action hinges on that fatal letter: there it is, in the letter box; and when Helmer opens it he will discover all about Nora's forgery. She is dressed up in Spanish finery for the fancy dress ball upstairs, and she tries to distract her husband's attention from the letter box by demanding an immediate rehearsal of her party piece, the tarantella. On one level this is straightforward plotting in the manner of Scribe, who was fond of catastrophic letters; the action is delayed, and the suspense is terrible. And even within the limits of the real situation portrayed on the stage there is ample scope for the exercise of Ibsen's irony. We see Nora dressed for a party when she feels more fit for a funeral —it is even called a masquerade. There is pathos, too: Nora the woman who has always been treated as a child, reacts with a characteristically childish evasion of the issue; she knows she can only postpone the dreadful moment, but even a brief postponement is worth every ounce of effort she can put into it.

Obviously the sequence where Nora dances the tarantella would be highly dramatic even if we only apprehended the "real" elements in the charade. But there is also a grim *double entente*. The tarantella, we remember, is supposed to be a cure for the bite of the tarantula spider; the dancer dances in order to work the poison out of his system before it kills him. Nora's dance has associations that are applied to Nora's situation. From the point of view of the realism of the piece, she might as well perform some entirely different dance; but

obviously the tarantella is appropriate, quite apart from the fact that it gives the actress playing Nora every chance to appear distracted. There is an aura about the tarantella that makes us see Nora and her predicament in a sinister light.

Allusions of this kind are frequent in *A Doll's House*. They act as windows in the realistic set, serving either to give a glimpse of the outside world, so as to place the action in a wider context, or else to let in light that illuminates the detail within. The tarantella is firmly anchored in the story, and its evocative function is only secondary; but Ibsen was not above putting in a sequence for the sole purpose of making an allusion of this kind. The best example I can call to mind comes in *The Wild Duck*. Gregers Werle takes a room with the Ekdals, and he proves an untidy tenant: he lights a fire in his stove, but forgets to open the vent, so the room is filled with smoke; then he tries to mend matters by pouring the water from his washstand over the fire, covering the floor with water and wet ashes; and, finally, he goes out for a walk, leaving the mess for someone else to clear up. This is obviously intended as a character sketch of Gregers; his attempt to foist his ideals on the Ekdal family has a much more disastrous effect, in the suicide of Hedvig, but the general pattern of behaviour is the same. Greger's mishap with the stove does nothing to forward the plot, and has even been called unrealistic. But the incident has a perfectly clear meaning in its context, and certainly does not lead to any sort of confusion or ambiguity.

If this sort of thing can be called "symbolism" at all—and a quick glance at the critical literature about Ibsen will convince one that it can—then it is at least symbolism in the manner of a David Low cartoon rather than of Maeterlinck or Rimbaud. There is nothing obscure about the works of Ibsen's middle period. It is true that his allusions may conjure up complex vistas of associations, all more or less relevant to the situation of the play; but this is exceptional

—more often he uses a straightforward *double entente*—and in any case the relevance of any allusion is always defined and limited by the narrative. For instance, the tarantula's victim presumably dances in the hope of ridding himself finally of the spider's poison, but the suggested analogy does not lead us to see Nora's dance as a possible solution of her difficulties. Her predicament is given depth and colour by means of the allusion, but it is defined by the realistic story.

But when we come to Ibsen's last plays, the ones that are always called symbolic, the method may at first appear quite different. The allusions in the plays of Ibsen's middle period are significant by virtue of their narrative context; and it may be argued that in a play like *The Master Builder* the necessary context is lacking. The allusive, evocative language is there—all sorts of parallels are suggested; but the play does not have a strong simple narrative framework in terms of which these vague allusions may acquire any precise meaning. The main narrative, in *The Master Builder*, seems as much in need of definition as anything else.

There are commentators who are ready to believe that Ibsen has simply overreached himself, that he has been so intent on making his words carry a multiplicity of meanings that he has become, in the end, incoherent. But this is not so. It is true that any résumé of the plot of *The Master Builder* tends to sound a little zany, but this is precisely because a brief statement of the events of the play leaves out the context that gives these events significance. In fact the play is a model of precision; but it is no longer the narrative thread that binds it together. The unity of *The Master Builder* depends on the analogous motives of the various characters, which give the whole play an impetus in a single direction. To elucidate the play, to point out its felicities, is not so much a task for the literary critic at all; it is a matter for the producer of the play, who has the opportunity to lay the stresses where they belong, so as to allow the symmetry of the whole to emerge.

The very first line of the play requires particular emphasis, as Ibsen's stage directions indicate. The curtain rises on the drawing office where Knut and Ragnar Brovik and Kaja Fosli are discovered at work. All three work in silence for some while. Then old Knut Brovik suddenly starts out of his chair, and moves forwards towards the audience, nervously tense and breathing with difficulty. His line is: "I can't bear this much longer!" Brovik's motive is immediately and forcefully established: he wants a show-down with the boss, Solness. Later we discover that he wants his son Ragnar to be allowed to undertake a building job on his own; Solness will not give the job away, and Brovik retires frustrated. This incident is used to illustrate Solness's fear of being superseded by the younger generation, and it has a purpose as an element in the plot. But its immediate effect is to create a mood. We at once respond to old Brovik's sense of frustration, and his feeling that the situation is no longer bearable, that matters must be brought to a head straight away.

The scenes that follow are mainly expository; and then, suddenly, Hilde Wangel bursts into the room like a young volcano. She is full of life and impertinence, as different as she possibly could be from the dispirited Broviks. But after a while it appears that she, too, has come to demand a show-down. She has her peculiar story of a kingdom that Solness is supposed to have promised her ten years ago. At the time Solness had just finished building the new church at Lysanger, and had placed the wreath on the completed spire with his own hand. Afterwards he met Hilde, then a thirteen-year-old schoolgirl; and she says that he kissed her and promised her that she was to be his princess when she grew up; in ten years' time he would give her a kingdom. Now the ten years are up, and she has come walking across the mountain to collect. Come on,

Master Builder, out with the promised
land!

Hilde's gay demand is a restatement of
the opening theme in a major key. The
very fact that her story sounds so unlikely,
that Solness has absolutely no recollection
of the promise he is supposed to have made,
only strengthens the dramatic force of her
purpose. And at this point the whole play
slides into gear. For although Solness does
not really know what Hilde is talking about,
and half suspects that she is simply kidding
him, yet he finds himself responding to her,
he can understand her language. The fact is
that in the light of Hilde's absurd story Solness is able to see his own purpose clearly
for the first time.

Solness is not a happy man. He has been
outstandingly successful as a builder, but it
seems to him that he has paid for his success with absolutely everything that makes
life worth living. His success was largely
a result of a fire that burned his wife's
parental home; but the same fire caused the
death of his baby twins, and gave his wife
a shock from which she never fully recov-
ered. We discover that on the occasion of
which Hilde speaks, when he climbed the
spire of the church at Lysanger, Solness
had made an oath that he would never build
a church again. It appeared to him that God
had deprived him of his children so that he
could continue to build churches; and Solness stood at the top of the spire and asserted his defiance of God. Since that time
he has built only dwelling houses, and his
success has been enormous; but it still appears to him that he has been somehow
cheated of his destiny.

This, then, is Solness's condition when
Hilde comes along to demand her kingdom.
And he finds that he can respond to the account she gives of herself. For him, too, that
morning at Lysanger held the promise of a
new kingdom. At that moment, ten years
ago, everything seemed possible, he stood
at the beginning of a new career as an independent creator in his own field; and now
for ten years the promise has been unful-

filled. He finds a fresh inspiration in Hilde's
youthful enthusiasm, and he determines to
make his demand on life once again, to enter into the promised land.

The way in which Ibsen depicts the final
working out of Solness's resolve is bold in
the extreme. Solness has always been afraid
of heights, and has only once overcome
his fear—when he climbed the spire of the
church. Now he determines to do "the impossible" once again: he will place the
wreath on the completed tower of his new
house himself. He carries out the feat; he is
overcome with dizziness, and he falls to his
death. On the face of it this resolution of
the play is no resolution at all: Solness's
attempt to overcome his dizziness has no
rational connexion with the problem he is
trying to face. But Ibsen's art does not depend only on rational connexions. Solness's ascent of the tower carries all sorts
of overtones: he wants to regain the moment of complete clarity that he enjoyed at
Lysanger, he wants to master his fate once
again; and in the emotional context that
has been created his purpose is clear, and
his action is perfectly credible.

If Gregers's encounter with his stove in
The Wild Duck can properly be called
"symbolic" (which is rather doubtful),
then there is some sense in calling The Master Builder a symbolic play. For here the
whole story of Solness's frustration and his
determination to overcome his innate dizziness is the exact analogue of Gregers's
misadventure: it is a presentation of the
action of the play in what I can only call
caricature. In its way the caricature is
masterly. Ibsen is anatomizing a peculiar
specis of motive, and his representation hits
off the features of his original most tell-
ingly.

I have attempted, briefly, to pick out the
main line of the play's development; and
my analysis has necessarily left most of The
Master Builder entirely unexplored. I hope
I have said enough to illustrate my main
point: that while Ibsen's earlier plays are
built round a realistic narrative, the last

plays are organized in quite a different manner. In *The Master Builder* the theme is briefly introduced in the entirely realistic episode with Knut Brovik; and it is then boldly underlined in Hilde Wangel's claim, which shows us the central theme of the play, the demand for the promised kingdom, in its simplest and clearest form, divorced from any realistic motivational history. Finally the theme is explored in depth in the audaciously impressionistic portrayal of Solness. The main narrative thread of the play, which shows us Solness's growing determination to climb the tower of his new house and his subsequent fall, is itself a sort of caricature of the theme; the defining context, that gives the caricature its precise significance, is supplied by the analogous motives of the lesser characters on a more readily accessible level.

Ibsen used this same method of definition by analogy, with only slight variations, in all his later plays at least from *Hedda Gabler* onwards. It was a method eminently suited to dramatic presentations. It did not merely free him from the tiresome inanities of the well-made plot. It also gave him the size of canvas he needed for his dramatic explorations: he could project his subject simultaneously in as many forms as he required; and it gave him a great deal of freedom from the limitations of the realistic stage—he could adopt very stylized and sophisticated modes of expression. Above all, it enabled him to achieve a unique detachment from his characters; as his subject was no longer defined by a single character in a particular situation, like Mrs. Alving in *Ghosts,* he no longer needed to rely on a particular sympathetic response.

Critics sometimes deplore the ambivalence of attitude that is betrayed in Ibsen's plays, and this ambivalence is nowhere more apparent than in his last work. But the ironic—if you like, equivocal—attitude of mind that is characteristic of Ibsen as a playwright was also an essential condition of his art. It seems to me that Ibsen's last plays, which embody his most daring technical innovations, also constitute his most significant contribution to our self-knowledge.

Arthur Miller

The "Real" in Ibsen's Realism

WHEN *All My Sons* opened on Broadway it was called an "Ibsenesque" play. Some people liked it for this reason and others did not. Ibsen is relevant to this play but what he means to me is not always what he means to others, either his advocates or his detractors. More often than not, these days, he is thought of as a stage carpenter with a flair for ideas of importance. The whole aim of shaping a dramatic work on strict lines which will elicit a distinct meaning reducible to a sentence is now suspect. "Life" is now more complicated than such a mechanical contrasting of forces can hope to reflect. Instead, the aim is a "poetic" drama, preferably one whose ultimate thought or meaning is elusive, a drama which appears not to have been composed or constructed, but which somehow comes to life on a stage and then flickers away. To come quickly to the point, our theater inclines toward the forms of adolescence rather than analytical adulthood. . . .

To return to Ibsen's influence upon this play, I should have to split the question in order to make sense of it. First, there was the real impact of his work upon me at the time: this consisted mainly in what I then saw as his ability to forge a play upon a factual bedrock. A situation in his plays is never stated but revealed in terms of hard actions, irrevocable deeds; and sentiment is never confused with the action it conceals. Having for so long written in terms of what people felt rather than what they did, I turned to his works at the time with a sense of homecoming. As I have said, I wanted then to write so that people of common sense would mistake my play for life itself and not be required to lend it some poetic license before it could be believed. I wanted to make the moral world as real and evident as the immoral one so splendidly is.

But my own belief is that the shadow of Ibsen was seen on this play for another reason, and it is that *All My Sons* begins very late in its story. Thus, as in Ibsen's best-known work, a great amount of time is taken up with bringing the past into the present. In passing, I ought to add that this view of action is presently antipathetic to our commonly held feeling about the drama. More than any other quality of realism, or, to be more exact, of Ibsenism as a technique, this creates a sense of artificiality which we now tend to reject, for in other respects realism is still our reigning style. But it is no longer acceptable that characters should sit about discussing events of a year ago, or ten years ago, when in "life" they would be busy with the present. In truth, the effort to eliminate antecedent material has threatened to eliminate the past entirely from many plays. We are impatient to get on with it—so much so that anyone making a study of some highly creditable plays of the moment would be hard put to imagine what their characters were like a month before their actions and stories begin. *All My Sons* takes its time with the past, not in deference to Ibsen's method as I saw it then, but because its theme is the question of actions and consequences, and a way had to be found to throw a long line into the past to make the kind of connection viable. . . .

But before I leave this play it seems wise

to say a few more words about the kind of dramatic impulse it represents, and one aspect of "Ibsenism" as a technique is the quickest path into that discussion. I have no vested interest in any one form—as the variety of forms I have used attests—but there is one element in Ibsen's method which I do not think ought to be overlooked, let alone dismissed as it so often is nowadays. If his plays, and his method, do nothing else they reveal the evolutionary quality of life. One is constantly aware, in watching his plays, of process, change, development. I think too many modern plays assume, so to speak, that their duty is merely to show the present countenance rather than to account for what happens. It is therefore wrong to imagine that because his first and sometimes his second acts devote so much time to a studied revelation of antecedent material, his view is static compared to our own. In truth, it is profoundly dynamic, for that enormous past was always heavily documented to the end that the present be comprehended with wholeness, as a moment in a flow of time, and not—as with so many modern plays—as a situation without roots. Indeed, even though I can myself reject other aspects of his work, it nevertheless presents barely and unadorned what I believe is the biggest single dramatic problem, namely, how to dramatize what has gone before. I say this not merely out of technical interest, but because dramatic characters, and the drama itself, can never hope to attain a maximum degree of consciousness unless they contain a viable unveiling of the contrast between past and present, and an awareness of the process by which the present has become what it is. And I say this, finally, because I take it as a truth that the end of drama is the creation of a higher consciousness and not merely a subjective attack upon the audience's nerves and feelings. What is precious in the Ibsen method is its insistence upon valid causation, and this cannot be dismissed as a wooden notion.

This is the "real" in Ibsen's realism for me, for he was, after all, as much a mystic as a realist. Which is simply to say that while there are mysteries in life which no amount of analyzing will reduce to reason, it is perfectly realistic to admit and even to proclaim that hiatus as a truth. But the problem is not to make complex what is essentially explainable; it is to make understandable what is complex without distorting and oversimplifying what cannot be explained. I think many of his devices are, in fact, quite arbitrary; that he betrays a Germanic ponderousness at times and a tendency to overprove what is quite clear in the first place. But we could do with more of his basic intention, which was to assert nothing he had not proved, and to cling always to the marvelous spectacle of life forcing one event out of the jaws of the preceding one and to reveal its elemental consistencies with surprise. In other words, I contrast his realism not with the lyrical, which I prize, but with sentimentality, which is always a leak in the dramatic dike. He sought to make a play as weighty and living a fact as the discovery of the steam engine or algebra. This can be scoffed away only at a price, and the price is a living drama.

Ronald Peacock

Effects of Ibsen

"YES, Ibsen is ugly, common, hard, prosaic, bottomlessly bourgeois—and with his distinction so far *in*, as it were, so behind doors and beyond vestibules, that one is excusable for not pushing one's way to it. And yet of his art he's a master—and I feel in him, to the pitch of almost intolerable boredom, the presence and the insistence of life. On the other hand, his mastery, so bare and lean as it is, wouldn't count nearly as much in any medium in which the genus was otherwise represented. In *our* sandy desert even this translated octopus (excuse my comparison of habitats!!) sits alone, and isn't kept in his place by relativity." So Henry James wrote in a letter to Julian Sturgis in 1893. Ibsen was one of those artists whose work divides people from the first between admiration and hostility. Not every artist does this; it is not the infallible criterion of originality; and it is not simply a question of a novel inspiration that is in advance of its time and comes later to be accepted. People of mature and discriminating taste, not ignoramuses, separated into opposite camps over Ibsen's work, or, like James, felt there was a doubt. It was precisely what happened with another great artist of the nineteenth century, Wagner, especially in regard to his *Tristan and Isolde*. In such cases it is true that in one sense time and familiarity soften the harshness of the first opposition, and the work establishes some sort of position for itself. But it is also true that the division of opinion, the fundamental disunity of aesthetic judgement in connection with it, continues; often in the form of a conflict

in one's own mind. Nietzsche and Thomas Mann perpetually succumb to the "diabolical" fascination of *Tristan and Isolde* and perpetually cast suspicion on the sources of it and that part of themselves that responds. When this happens it is because the work itself does in fact raise some profound issue concerning the nature of art and its relation to human values.

The "social problem" plays of Ibsen are in this category and their influence will be the main topic of this essay. The difficulty of approaching Ibsen, of getting to like and admire him and acquire a fair judgement about him, is due to the disproportionate importance of the social plays. They are only a part, and a relatively small one, of his work; but they are the part that made him a European force. Younger people cannot feel directly, as older critics still do, what Ibsen's challenge meant and the powerful impact he made on European opinion. A proper understanding of it can now only be obtained by a laborious process of reconstruction which involves, I think, a very willing exercise of the historical sense and also reading a great deal of the writing about him that was contemporaneous with productions of his works. For the appreciation of his work as a whole, and for our present approach to him, the separation of the social plays from the rest has been unfortunate to a degree, although it was inevitable. Can it be said that appreciation of Ibsen's work as a whole has even begun?

There were in Ibsen from his earliest period two very powerful forces, one an

From *The Poet in the Theatre* by Ronald Peacock. Copyright 1946, copyright © 1960 by Ronald Peacock. Reprinted by permission of Hill and Wang, Inc., New York, and Routledge & Kegan Paul, Ltd., London.

overriding passion for Truth, or perhaps rather Truthfulness, and the other an exceptional sense of dramatic situation based on the interplay of character.

By temperament he was an idealist, but an idealist with only one ideal. If others evade facts and become romantics of illusion, Ibsen faced them and became a romantic of Truthfulness. Many have seen what they term a new "classicism" in his drama, meaning apparently an objective picture of life and a strict analytical technique. But below the surface, and below the superficial German romanticism of the early plays, it may be that Ibsen is profoundly romantic, possibly in fact the great belated dramatist of the whole romantic movement. He used drama to present in impersonal terms a personal struggle. Like Racine and Shakespeare he was a master of an extensive range of character-portrayal; but whilst their protagonists give a cumulative picture of Man, his repeat the picture of the rebel against society, in the sense of integrity against hypocrisy, of independence against cowardice, of spiritual vitality against deadening convention. He creates a myth of the Truthful Man, and the settings of his plays show a drama of symbolism to drive home the ideal. The vistas of fiords and hills, the boats going to sea, the steeples and mountain-tops, all there to lure his principal characters away from society, into the free distance, out into a clean natural air, upwards to a rarefied unpolluted sphere, to a solitude for strong spirits—they all mark the freedom that is consonant with the achievement of his personal ideal; and they mark too, often tragically, the separation of the ideal from life.

The other powerful force in Ibsen's work was, as indicated above, his interest in dramatic situation. The excitement of a rapidly moving plot and of dynamic events is a part of his drama, and it is invariably built up on the basis of a compact and full picture of character and life. But its most original aspect is an extraordinary sense of precipitated crisis. His situations portray the quintessence of crisis and they seem to have been shaped under the compulsion of an acute emotional response to the utmost concentration of conflict and tension. In Ibsen this has the character of a primary poetic experience. It is an immediate feeling for the dramatic as a phenomenon of life, a sensuous, almost mystical contact with the very concept of drama, over and above the particular details of persons and events in which it appears. He is always a master of such detail; but in play after play he transcends it and communicates a sense at once emotional and abstract of the pure dramatic. He is the supreme artist of the dramatic, and his name has become symbolic wherever the essentials of the art are inquired into.

Of the two strains thus singled out for brief comment, the latter is directly evident in the historical plays, *The Vikings at Helgeland* and *The Pretenders*, where it has the field to itself. In most of the other plays there is a varying interfusion of the two. In earlier ones, *Love's Comedy*, for instance, or *Brand,* the sense of personal statement is predominant. In the period that opens with *Pillars of Society*, the two are in powerful conjunction, though the idealism of truth takes the impersonal form of a remorseless analysis of motives and "ideals" in social living. The last phase, from *Hedda Gabler* on (though *Rosmersholm* is on the borderline), shows a similar combination, but the personal theme is now transformed into a study of the perversion of originality, of the canker in the rose, of the character in whom the creative free independent truthful spirit is distorted by the demonic, assailing from within or without: Hedda, Solness, Borkman, Rubek.

In his histories, in the plays with an almost autobiographical element, *Brand* and *Peer Gynt*, in the plays of the last period, Ibsen is most dramatic and most poetic at one and the same time. The work of the middle period is highly dramatic, but the creative imagination is subordinated to a critical analysis in the cause of truthfulness.

It is the work that had an immense influence on the drama in Europe.

Under the impact of this subject-matter that had a pronounced contemporary interest, a controversial value, and a social application, writing and production in the English theatre burst into a great efflorescence; and yet the movement failed to produce the great dramatic literature. That is the remarkable fact and the critical problem. The novelty and immediacy of the subject-matter, and the conscientious temper of the new writers, were clearly notable and warranted all the excitement they caused. It seemed that the theatre was being liberated effectively from stereotyped entertainment, and art rescued from the aestheticism of the "nineties"; and if vitality is to be measured by these things and by extent of production and imitation, the new type of play would certainly claim that quality. It attained a front position for itself. For a generation the most widely accepted notion of what a good play should be was a thoughtful play for thoughtful people. From Shaw and Granville Barker, through eminent and minor playwrights alike, and not forgetting the timely assistance of reflective rational Euripides, who was played as often as anyone else, down to a recent work like *Thunder Rock*, in which we see a last low ebbing of the tide, the type has dominated the stage and criticism.

Looking back now on the period that produced *The Voysey Inheritance* and *Candida*, *Loyalties* and *The Skin Game*, *Outward Bound* and *A Bill of Divorcement*, *Young Woodley* and *The Vortex*, *Robert's Wife* and *Dangerous Corner*, it is incredible that it should ever have been called "great." All these plays are competent, some of them excellent; all of them are representative plays of ideas, all successes of their time. Nevertheless they can attract now but little critical interest. The phenomenon as a whole, however, the drama *à thèse* reigning for thirty years in a royal state, is of acute interest for a critical history of drama. The type had been known before, but it had never held sway over the very conception of drama, never been glorified into the pattern of dramatic perfection. It is worth while trying to find an explanation of how a period went wrong when it did so on such a grand scale.

The explanation lies in Ibsen's middle phase, the principal feature of which is that a very powerful dramatic technique coincided with a general wave of social thinking. Ibsen, as we have recalled, treated a variety of subjects in the course of his career. His great range is part of his distinction; the social subject was only one of his lines. But it was of the highest significance that he turned to social subjects in a period when his technical powers had reached their height. Advanced thought in Europe was already directed to social problems; the drama was debilitated; the combination in Ibsen of social interest and great new dramatic power produced the impressive new creation. The "serious" drama, the didactic social problem play was launched under the best conceivable auspices. It was a tremendous success; it was blindly imitated; it possessed the theatre.

Ibsen's work was, and to some extent still is, extraordinarily deceptive because of the sheer technical skill he displayed. But he had developed it in the plays he wrote previously to his social dramas. And those gave him much more genuine poetry than the dialectic of beliefs or the critical diagnosis of social habits could. Through this development, however, he obtained a degree of craftsmanship that enabled him to handle the social subject-matter in a masterly fashion. He gives every appearance of having met successfully the difficulties caused by its casuistic inspiration. Applying the massive technique that he had nourished from quite different roots, he made the new drama plausible as art. To this piece of virtuosity was due the new movement in the theatre, the establishment of a new ideal of what drama should be and do.

The detached spectator of today can more

easily see how the social problem plays of Ibsen do not compare for artistic unity with his earlier or later work. One can readily admit admiration of the degree to which Ibsen, hammering—according to the familar picture—at his material, working out in months of contemplation at his desk the "biographies" of his characters, does impose some kind of unity; admiration of the way in which he fits to his moral analysis persons and situations conceived so skilfully that they have a great semblance of naturalness, sometimes even of inevitability. But can one forget for long the double purpose? The dissociation between a "message" and an artistic apparatus is not to be hidden. The curtains of the first two acts of *Ghosts*—Mrs. Alving catching sight of Oswald kissing the maid, and the burning of the orphanage—are examples of a kind of artificiality that comes from moral and social difficulties being focused by the manipulation of persons and circumstances.

Archer, the pure critic, saw the defect in this hybrid between opinion and art, and he seems to have regretted that what he rightly considered Ibsen's best work was not his most influential. Pure criticism was not the forte of the play-writing disciples, or of the "serious" public that acclaimed them. They seem not to have had the acuteness that enabled Archer to see where Ibsen was great as a social critic and where he was great as an artist. They seem to have overestimated the usefulness of the real conflict their drama took for its subject, arguing perhaps in this way: Conflict is the essence of drama, therefore conflict transferred to the stage will be good drama. Only such a misjudgement explains the anxiety to imitate Ibsen. Their imitations, however, show how much in him was due to the special use of an extraordinary equipment; how the type of social problem play launched by Ibsen, having its real origin in ratiocination and debate, rests on false foundations by comparison with the tradition of drama and with Ibsen's own best. Without the master's personal force, his conscience and his challenge, this type shows up at once as an aberration. Ibsen himself abandoned it.

It was through Ibsen, therefore, that the idea of drama was standardized as an analysis of conflicting social and moral attitudes cast in the mould of tragedy or near-tragedy. The essentially practical inspiration of such a drama—the changing of manners and institutions—induced the highest respect for "realism." Analysis found its usefulness enhanced in proportion as it grew more and more *exact*, more and more photographic. Literal truthfulness to life was the soul of the diagnosis. The very impulse of this drama eliminates the poetic imagination. The master himself tells us that in his social dramas he had to get more "prosaic," closer to "reality"; we believe him, he knew what he was about. His imitators, whilst they had no need of making any such sacrificial descent, spread themselves in the prosaic realism that dried up poetry and style at the roots. It was a boast of the time, pardonable enough in relation to stock theatrical entertainment, that drama had achieved its "intellectual freedom." The price paid for this distinction was its poetic life.

Thus Ibsen's liberation of drama was not, when we consider the results in England, so advantageous or so unquestionable as many have held. A very powerful writer had a very wrong influence.

It is to the credit of this body of drama that it was undoubtedly contemporary in spirit, even though it often was so in an obvious if not superficial way. To ignore the romantic and pseudo-poetic and try to discover new foundations in a social theme relevant to the life of the day was a sign of vitality. But it was only one half the task of art.

The artistic failure of the social problem drama makes one ponder its relation to the art for art's sake movement to which in its early stages it was consciously opposed. The new dramatists accused the aesthetes of sterility because they were remote from life. The artists might very well reverse the accusation and say that the playwrights might have contact with life but were remote from art. It is amusing to reflect at this distance that in one sense the aesthetes come out of it rather better, since they at any rate didn't pretend, although they could be good at pretending, to have a great social message for whole communities, whereas the people with the social interest did pretend to have art. Every art has objective conditions which might be modified by new subject-matter but cannot be ignored; hence tradition. The writers of social problem drama, misled by the example of one phase of Ibsen's work, did neglect the conditions of art, and so produced a body of work that may have been influential and successful at a certain level, but lacked poetic distinction.